clued up

ARE YOU

ATTEN

PAYING
TION?

clued up

working through politics and complexity

Alan Robertson
Graham Abbey

www.yourmomentum.com
the stuff that drives you

What is momentum?

Momentum is a completely new publishing philosophy, in print and online, dedicated to giving you more of the information, inspiration and drive to enhance who you are, what you do, and how you do it.

Fusing the changing forces of work, life and technology, momentum will give you the bright stuff for a brighter future and set you on the way to being all you can be.

Who needs momentum?

Momentum is for people who want to make things happen in their career and their life, who want to work at something they enjoy and that's worthy of their talent and their time.

Momentum people have values and principles, and question who they are, what they do, and who for. Wherever they work, they want to feel proud of what they do. And they are hungry for information, stimulation, ideas and answers ...

Momentum online

Visit *www.yourmomentum.com* to be part of the talent community. Here you'll find a full listing of current and future books, an archive of articles by momentum authors, sample chapters and self-assessment tools. While you're there, post your worklife questions to our momentum coaches and sign up to receive free newsletters with even more stuff to drive you.

More momentum

If you need more drive for your life, try one of these titles, all published under the momentum label:

change activist
make big things happen fast
Carmel McConnell

lead yourself
be where others will follow
Mick Cope

happy mondays
putting the pleasure back into work
Richard Reeves

the big difference
life works when you choose it
Nicola Phillips

hey you!
pitch to win in an ideas economy
Will Murray

snap, crackle or stop
change your career and create your own destiny
Barbara Quinn

float you
how to capitalize on your talent
Carmel McConnell & Mick Cope

innervation
redesign yourself for a smarter future
Guy Browning

from here to e
equip yourself for a career in the wired economy
Lisa Khoo

coach yourself
make real change in your life
Tony Grant & Jane Greene

grow your human capital
what you know, who you know, how you use it
Hilarie Owen

PEARSON EDUCATION LIMITED

Head Office
Edinburgh Gate
Harlow CM20 2JE
Tel: +44 (0)1279 623623
Fax: +44 (0)1279 431059

London Office:
128 Long Acre
London WC2E 9AN
Tel: +44 (0)20 7447 2000
Fax: +44 (0)20 7240 5771
Website: www.business-minds.com

First published in Great Britain in 2002

The right of Graham Abbey and Alan
Robertson to be identified as authors of this
work has been asserted by them in
accordance with the Copyright, Designs and
Patents Act 1988.

ISBN 1843 04014 X

British Library Cataloguing in Publication Data
A CIP catalogue record for this book can be
obtained from the British Library.

10 9 8 7 6 5 4 3 2 1

Typeset by Northern Phototypesetting Co. Ltd,
Bolton
Printed and bound in Great Britain by Biddles
Ltd, Guildford and King's Lynn

Production design by Claire Brodmann
Book Designs, Lichfield, Staffs.

The Publishers' policy is to use paper
manufactured from sustainable forests.

thank you…

everybody who has helped us to turn an idea into a book…

Hilary, Kate, Elie (our title-generator) and Brenda for reading the drafts and not being afraid to give us their feedback

Katie, for doing some of the jazz research and, with Mark, for keeping the book in perspective

Caitlin

David Perkins and Daniel Wilson at Harvard Project Zero for allowing us to use ideas on thinking and jazz, including their phrase 'the idea-action gap'

All those other people, some of them referenced in the book, whose ideas have influenced us

'Kim', 'Carl', 'Mattie', 'Saheena' and 'Malcolm' for sharing their learning experiences from the Networker project

Rachael, for taking on an idea when it was still on the wrong side of the gap

and last, but not least, thanks to each other (oh yuk!)

introduction

So what's this all about then?

Are you paying attention? Not just listening, but really paying attention to what's going on around you? Not surprising if you're not. It's increasingly difficult to pay attention in today's world because there is so much going on – the pace at which information comes at us is phenomenal, voice, print, text, video, SMS, broadband, blah, blah, blah.

It's noisy out there....

It is not just a question of paying attention, but knowing what to look for and where. We all have limited attention, so we should choose carefully how to invest it. It may be the scarcest resource we have.

Being effective is about making the right decisions at the right time. 20:20 hindsight is much less useful. How often do you realize what to do just *after* the moment when you needed to do it? A bummer, isn't it? But the information we need is there, all the time. There are clues. They need interpreting, judgements still need to be made, but first you have to spot them.

Get clued up.

This book is about how.

But we need to get one thing straight from the word go. This book does not contain any right answers. We don't believe in them. We don't believe in wrong ones either. Your world is too complex for any 'seven step plan' to hold all the ways forward. But this is good news. No, really. It gives you choice, it puts you in control. You can take the route to success that works for you, not be left worrying what was the seventh 'S' in the '7 S Model'.

So how will this book help?

While outright answers should be treated with caution, there are approaches to situations that, in our experience, help find a path that works for you in your situation. These are generally simple ideas that will help you read your situation more fully, interpret it more deeply and give you the confidence to take action and to learn from it.

The content of the chapters will give you something to hold on to as you face life in the messy modern organization. Things to allow you to shape your world and enable clearer, more effective choices to be made.

So, more specifically, how does this work?

This is a 'book of two halves', intertwined. There is a series of 'angles'. Each represents a particular view or perspective through which you can examine your situation. Every angle contains an idea or two, the odd model to help simplify the mess.

We have chosen the angles pragmatically. They are not designed to fit a unifying model so that humanity can be represented in a single page with a few boxes and arrows. We have chosen them because we have found them useful, as have the people with whom we have worked. You may find inconsistencies between them and between these particular angles and your own approaches. If you do, take it as a good sign. It means you are starting to make sense of these ideas in your context.

Unfortunately good learning is not just about absorbing high-level ideas that neatly ignore or at least gloss over real-life messiness. How many models do you think you know? With the explosion of professional and management training over the past decade, more than you need, we suspect. These organizers of thought play an important role, helping to simplify otherwise-too-complex situations, but you have to integrate these into your everyday activity for them to become useful.

This is the hard bit. It needs you to work on it. (Sorry!) We have provided help or at least encouragement, asking you to apply the ideas we present to your situation. Doing some of this will help. This is such a vital area, the application of ideas to your specific context, we have provided a working example throughout the book. This is a story. A real one. It is as important as the angles.

The 'episodes' are taken from interviews with a group of real people working together to launch a business idea. They are 'live data', although each person's story is filtered through their memory and may leave out details that another thought was important. Not initially your situation, although you may recognize similarities. As in real life, it is sometimes ambiguous and less conclusive than we might like. We can't offer you neat 'Hollywood' conclusions (the boy doesn't get the girl in the end!), but you may find it difficult not to become absorbed in the story.

The characters have been disguised and the choice of extracts is ours, selected to give you a chance to apply the angles to a particular context. Ask any one of the participants and they are likely, quite legitimately, to place the emphasis in some other way or reach different conclusions.

Remember, though, that the objective of the episodes is to provide a context for the angles, to help you develop your ability to spot clues.

As the book progresses we encourage you to move from our story to your story. You will see us referring to the episode material less and asking more questions of you. Asking you to think about your own situation. We will also distinguish less between individual angles, supporting you to think about them together, reflecting on their interrelationships. The final episode maps out a route through this messy territory. As we have said not a unifying theory to follow stepwise, but something to give you direction as you explore, to help you find a way that works for you and your situation. Our ideal outcome is that you leave this book with a coherent sense of what being clued up means for you (and, of course, wanting to recommend your friends to buy a copy too).

We encourage you to read the whole book (well, we would wouldn't we). The angles can be read in any order, but the story does unfold through the episodes. Different characters' perspectives are presented in each, so strictly you could choose to approach them out of sequence. If you do this, the story may take on the feel of a Tarantino film (but with less violence). If a guiding framework is what you like before entertaining the detail, you may enjoy starting with the final episode, our organizing framework. Go for what appeals.

A guiding principle for the book is that real effectiveness comes from knowing what to do in the moment, when faced with a baffling array of data to process. Therefore useful learning is what you can remember. You need to remember the things that give you most leverage, which will have most impact. Less is more.

It is customary to overview the chapters now. We would rather you dive in where you want. The contents page summarizes the subject matter.

So enter now. Go for it, enjoy.

idea-action gap

good thinking

complexity

An angle on complexity / 78

An episode on complexity / 98

politics

An angle on politics / 120

An episode on politics / 142

talking action

idea-action gap

an angle on
the idea action-gap
the real challenge of being personally effective

What's personal effectiveness all about?

Turning ideas into action.

So what's the problem?

There's a gap.

Mind the gap!

IDEA ... ... ACTION

It's a seductive notion, 'personal effectiveness'. Seductive because it's attractive and it leads us astray. It makes it sound as if being effective is just about the qualities of the person. Whether you have enough personal effectiveness or not.

But you can't be personally effective in a vacuum.

You can only gauge your effectiveness in relation to what you achieve. Which means that where and when you achieve become vital parts of the equation.

It's a matter of context.

We have to pay attention to context, because we need to be personally effective in the moment, in the flow of events, as we try to get things done in our jobs, in our careers and in our various life endeavours.

Situations such as when we're being interviewed for a job, or making a presentation to secure a contract, or putting an important point across when a decision hangs on the outcome. In the action, in the moment.

The problem is things are different in the moment

With hindsight we can all be personally effective. In the same way, after the event, we can all come up with the witty quip that we wish we'd been able to make at the time. It's not as if we don't know the sorts of things we have to do. There's masses of stuff on how to be personally effective. We're surrounded by advice on issues like how to structure our personal objectives and how to manage our time and how to develop our interpersonal skills. And the irony is that much of this advice is very good. It's not that we don't know what to do. The bigger problem is that much of the time we just don't use what we already know.

Why is that? Why is it so difficult for us to be personally effective when we need to be? A large part of the problem is that we miss the moment. Research suggests that up to 80 per cent of ineffective performance can be attributed not to a lack of know-how, or even to a lack of will, but rather to our failure to spot the requirement to call on the abilities we already have.

But why do we so often miss the moment? The problem is that the moment is a difficult place. Literally it's hard to catch. The moment is complex and noisy and difficult to categorize. The moment is not free-standing. It is always part of a complex of the various things that are going on at the same time. This makes it noisy and the more that is going on, the more people that are involved, the noisier it gets. Ever been in a meeting and had it on the tip of your tongue to make a particularly telling point only to hear the discussion veer off on a tangent before you got it out?

So the moment is fleeting. It is constantly prey to the stream of other moments that surround it and follow it and crowd it out. We don't get much time to spot the significant moment. It's like a passing glimpse of a face in a crowd. It's hard to put a name to it, and this makes it doubly difficult to recognize it for what it is, or what it might be. The clues are fleeting.

Not only is the moment a difficult place, but we ourselves are not well equipped for it. Our natural stock of attention is limited. And to make matters worse, we use up these attentional resources even more quickly when we are preoccupied with what we are doing, with an important task or something that matters a great deal to us. You know what it's like. You're concentrating hard on what someone's saying and you don't notice the unspoken reactions of other people round the table. Or vice versa. The effect is the same. Exactly when we need to be at our most alert to catch the moment, we can find ourselves most prone to miss it.

Of course this isn't always the case. When we're doing something that is familiar, the demands on our conscious attention are not so great. We have more left over because we've learned to do parts of the task automatically and unconsciously. But situations, roles, projects that require us to tackle something new or unfamiliar tax our attention heavily. So again, it is when the stakes are highest that we find ourselves most likely to miss the moment.

Ever been there? Think about it for a moment.

As often remarked, it's easy to make sense of life looking backwards – the difficulty is that we have to live it going forwards. And going forwards is messy. We need clues and an awareness of the sorts of clues to look for. The first place to look for them is in the idea-action gap because that is where the challenges to our personal effectiveness are situated and presented, moment by moment.

Why?

Because we spend our working lives trying to turn ideas into action. That's the stuff of how we spend our time.

Ideas of all shapes and sizes…

Maybe you've got the idea that you want to catch me and have a word before I go off on the trip that will have me out of the office for the next week. But you don't take account of all the other things I'm trying to do before I go, so you don't get to see me. You've got an idea that we could provide a better service by redesigning some of our processes. But although some people like your idea, there are one or two others you just don't seem to be able to persuade. You've got an idea that you'd like to change your career direction, start working more for yourself. But there's so much to consider, it keeps slipping.

These aren't just casual thoughts that we're happy to let go.

These are things that we want to achieve, that other people are looking to us to achieve. They may be projects to achieve tangible outcomes, such as inventions, designs, products or services, or more intangible projects, such as gaining support for a proposition, or understanding of an explanation. Likewise, ideas can vary enormously in scale, from designing the space shuttle or eliminating a disease to making an advertising poster, writing a song or getting our point across in a meeting. Tangible or intangible, large or small, all these endeavours require us to find and execute the actions that will translate our intention into an outcome.

So what is the gap?

Ask anyone. They'll give you an answer readily enough.

'Having an idea, but not being able to put it into practice.'

'Knowing what to do but not actually managing to do it.'

'Not making use of what we already know.'

'Taking action with a clear intention only to find that it produces unexpected outcomes.'

Are these the gap? Or are they just indications that the gap exists? They certainly don't explain the gap. They don't give us any clues to help us see it coming or avoid it before we tumble into it. So we need a clearer sense of what the gap consists of, and where to look for it, or we don't stand much chance of dealing with it.

The gap may seem obvious to you. If so, you may feel over the next few pages that we're labouring the point. However, please bear with it because there is much about the gap that is not obvious and needs to be understood.

It's a search for the unobvious.

One of the problems with the idea-action gap is that it isn't obvious until after the event. It's conspicuously inconspicuous. We've all sat in those post-mortem meetings, where the reasons why things didn't go according to plan are laid bare. We know the phrases. *'Well, I can see it now.' 'Yes, but I didn't know that at the time.' 'You never said.'* And we've all come out of other meetings where we've heard people saying, *'What was going on there?' 'Don't know. Beats me.'* Now there's a clue that an idea-action gap is just around the corner.

So here's a way of picturing it.

The idea-action gap is a hostile environment.

Think for a moment about other hostile environments.

Think of jungles. Filled with obvious obstructions that block your path and your view. Filled with unseen and unobvious threats, wild things, predators, noises and movements that we don't recognize. What can we touch? Where dare we step safely? The environment is filled with resources, but they are raw and unfamiliar, difficult to identify and to find. Which are useful and which are dangerous?

Think of deserts. The horizon is wide, but the resources to enable us to keep going are few and far between. And so are the landmarks. Where are we? How do we make out our destination? How can we mark our progress? It's hard even to move with the sand constantly slipping away beneath our feet. And it's hard to mark our progress when a wind can suddenly come upon us, seemingly from nowhere, and so easily wipe out our footprints.

Think of the polar regions. Sometimes it's easy to move when the ground beneath our feet is smooth and hard. We glide along. But at other times we are up to our knees, or deeper, in snow. Every step is a huge effort. And even when the way is easier, the surface is treacherous and unforgiving. It is easy to fall. A thin covering of snow may hide a deep crevasse. Or the ice can yawn and crack, opening suddenly and closing again.

What is it about these environments that makes them difficult?

Progress isn't easy. It isn't easy to see the way through, either because there is too much in the way or because there are too few features to guide us. What we can see we don't necessarily understand.

The environment is seldom stable. It's dynamic. It shifts and changes in ways that we find hard to predict. It is difficult to be prepared for it.

And consequently the environment is complex, both in itself and because it surpasses our understanding.

Are we dramatizing?

Yes and no. Of course we've chosen a dramatic metaphor to make our point. We want it to stick in your mind. We want it to make you alert to the existence of the idea-action gap. But is it over-dramatic? We think not.

Is the metaphor of a hostile environment an appropriate one for modern organizational and occupational life? We think so.

You have a project, a goal, a set of responsibilities to accomplish. Think about your own. How often is your way forward clear and unencumbered? On small tasks, the routine and the familiar, perhaps. But on the bigger projects, the ones that matter to you most, the obstacles are all too frequent. How many projects have you been involved in that went exactly and smoothly according to plan?

Just stop and think about that for a moment. Do you agree?

Obstacles and difficulties are part and parcel of our occupational lives. Yet they are not necessarily easily apparent.

Many of the pitfalls that we encounter are not immediately obvious. Consequences of our own actions that we failed to anticipate, for instance. People who raise no objection to our plan but resist its implementation in practice. Unexpected external developments that shift the goalposts, causing us to have to adjust our targets one way or another. Reactions from other people that come as a surprise.

So here are some quick yes/no questions…

◆ Is your way forward sometimes far from obvious?

◆ Do you sometimes feel unsure of what is going to happen?

◆ Are your surroundings – including, and perhaps especially, the people you have to deal with – sometimes unpredictable?

- Is it sometimes an effort to keep going?

- Is it sometimes difficult to make sense of what's going on around you?

- Do you have to work hard to shape your circumstances?

Do you live and work in an essentially hostile environment? You decide.

Is personal effectiveness in today's organizations and occupations a matter of being able to cross this sort of gap? We think so. That's what makes crossing the idea-action gap the acid test of personal effectiveness.

We're going to need to consider what sorts of behaviours are effective in a hostile environment, but before we do that let's get a better sense of what the gap looks like and how we experience it in our organizational and occupational lives.

Where to look for the idea-action gap

We've already established that one of the difficulties with the idea-action gap is that it's easy to see it after the event but harder to see it coming. We need to look for clues and we need to know the clues to look for. But where do we look? One of the problems is that the gap can have many different sources. Some are external, such as circumstances or other people, while others are internal to ourselves, such as the quality of our thinking or our attitude to risk. Because the sources of the gap can be so dispersed, a more immediately revealing question to ask is, *when* does the gap tend to occur? When do our ideas tend to fail to make it into action? Think about that for a minute and then compare your thoughts with the list we have developed. Read the list mindfully and see if you can recall an example of each.

When do ideas tend to fall into the gap?

- When the idea is new.

- When the idea is complex.

- When the idea has to be pursued over a long period of time.

- When circumstances change, or keep changing.

- When several people are involved.

- When people have difficulty understanding the idea, or each other.

- When people are apprehensive (or intolerant, not open-minded).

- When others simply don't comprehend our ideas.

- When others resist or oppose our ideas.

- When we don't see what's going on and get left behind by events.

- When we don't understand the implications of what's going on.

- When we persist with an approach that isn't working.

- When we can't generate options or room for movement.

- When we can see what needs to be done but prevaricate, hesitating to commit ourselves.

We don't claim that this list is comprehensive, but we think it's enough to make our point. *'When?'* is a question that produces many pointers. It also serves as a reminder that the gap is *in the moment*. But there is another pattern emerging from this list. Some of these 'whens' relate to the idea itself, others relate to external circumstances or other people, and yet others relate to us, to our actions or inaction. Idea, action, gap: all three elements are significant and we need to attend to them all.

How can you manage the idea-action gap?

Pursuing our earlier analogy, what sorts of behaviours are most useful in a hostile environment?

What makes Tarzan lord of the jungle? The fact that he knows his way around. He knows how to read the signs and comprehends what they signify. So being personally effective in a hostile environment involves being aware in the moment and understanding how situations are likely to unfold over time.

It's hard to be successful in a hostile environment, but not impossible. Above all it requires alertness.

You need to pick up the clues. That's why Eskimos have so many words for snow. That's why Lawrence of Arabia paid so much attention to the colours and textures of sand and rock. And it's the same in more everyday contexts. Experts make finer distinctions than novices. They are more sensitive to clues.

And they have a deeper appreciation of where those clues are pointing.

Which is what the angles in this book are about helping you to learn.

Crossing the idea-action gap is a learning process.

Making sense and using that sense. Learning and applying that learning. Crossing the idea-action gap requires that we know how to learn. Now, perhaps, help is at hand, since the learning cycle is one of the most widely described models in personal development.

There are several variations of the learning cycle concept, but they all follow a similar pattern. They suggest that we learn from activity and that, for our learning to be full and complete, we need to go through a series of phases: doing an activity, reviewing it, making sense of it and finally making use of the experience. The process is ongoing as we encounter new experiences.

You need fully to process the experience of any activity to turn it into learning.

idea-action gap

clued up

momentum

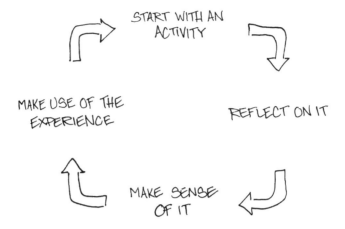

START WITH AN ACTIVITY

REFLECT ON IT

MAKE SENSE OF IT

MAKE USE OF THE EXPERIENCE

It is also recognized that, individually, we tend to have personal preferences, which lead us to put more energy and attention into certain aspects of the learning process and to neglect others. So some people prefer a hands-on approach, while others would rather watch and listen. Some want to be clear about the principles involved, while others like a checklist that lets them get on with it. You've probably seen all these approaches and their various combinations.

What is often suggested, more misleadingly, is that these are merely matters of 'style' and that learning can be done just as effectively in our preferred 'style', whether that be more active, more reflective, more theoretical or more practical. Our experience, however, is that reliance on particular learning style preferences makes ideas fall into the idea-action gap. We neglect the whole process at our peril.

A deeper understanding of the learning process

One of our observations about learning 'styles' is that people very often fall into one of two combinations of preference: either the 'try out and make use' or the 'reflect and make sense' patterns. This is where paying attention to some things and ignoring others can seriously interfere with being effective. In this case the result is a fracture in the learning process.

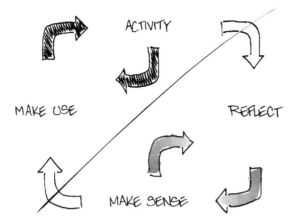

The significance of this fault line is readily apparent. Above the line the emphasis is on doing, on action. Below the line the emphasis is on thinking, on ideas. So here we have another example of the idea-action gap. But what may be even more important is where the fractures occur, because these are the clues to where our learning from experience tends to break down.

If you are clued up you pay attention to the points in the process where learning is most likely to be interrupted.

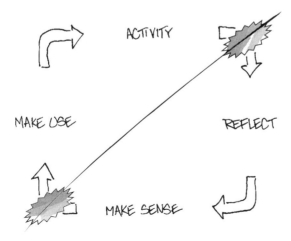

One of these fracture points is well known, the one that comes between making sense of something and actually using that understanding in practice. Failing to transfer knowing into doing. It's all too common. You will have seen it often enough. Just think, for example, of how often people fail to act on feedback.

The other fracture point, between experience and reflection, is perhaps less well known or less frequently noticed, but no less dangerous. It is an indicator of how often we fail to pause, even briefly, during our stream of activities in order to invest in the reflection that is necessary for effective learning. It shows our tendency to fail, in the moment.

Recognizing these fracture points can give us an important edge when we're trying to learn our way through a difficult environment. If we recognize them. That's why we need to be alert to clues.

So look out for these fracture points. Look out for the moment when something isn't working as you expected and you're tempted just to plunge in to trying something else. Look out for the moment when you think you've made sense of what's happening but you haven't thought through how you're going to use that insight.

Pay more attention to being reflective and to planning your actions.

Oh no, we hear you groan, don't these people understand that we don't have enough hours in the day as it is, without being asked to give more time to something else.

Yes, we understand that. So let's be clear about what we're saying.

Being personally effective is about turning ideas into action. Ideas often don't make it into action because the context in which we try to implement our ideas usually presents a lot of obstacles. We need to be active and thorough learners to get through this. But learning has to be done *in* the gap. Try to stand away from it and all you get is the thinking without the doing, and you're still stuck on the wrong side of the idea-action gap.

Turning ideas into action, like learning, involves both *thinking* and *doing*. One is of limited value without the other. We cannot be personally effective without both. Getting through the idea-action gap requires both active thinking and mindful action.

Priorities for attention and action

That's all very well, you say, but it still sounds as if you're asking us to commit more time and add more to what we already have to do.

No. What we're suggesting are some priorities which are broader, easier to bear in mind and more powerful in their impact.

We're saying, stay alert, stay mindful, keep moving, keep up your momentum. And in the demanding context of work these days it's easier to do this if you pay attention to clues in particular areas. Areas like the quality of your thinking, the complexity of your situation, the politics and your choice of words. These are the things that make the differences in the idea-action gap, so these are the subjects of this book.

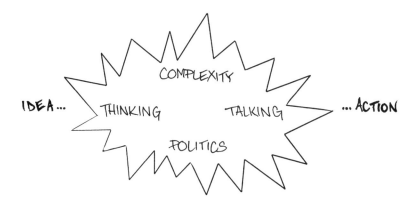

Remember, all the available advice on personal effectiveness is just not feasible. There's simply too much. The toolkit is so large and the moment is so fleeting.

And in any event, life doesn't present itself neatly labelled to fit the chapter titles of any book on personal effectiveness, this one included. The best we can hope for are clues. For which we had better be watchful.

So let's make it easier for ourselves. Let's drop the idea of toolkits. Drop the self-punishing belief that we have to be able to find exactly the right personal effectiveness tool to match the moment. Instead, let's adopt the broader – and certainly more easily remembered – notion that from moment to moment we have only two responsibilities: making sense of what's going on and making use of that sense. Sense making and shaping.

A wheel for your momentum, just keep on making sense and making use.

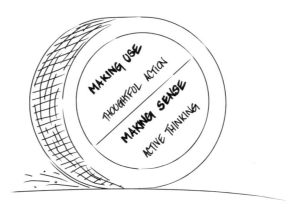

Making sense and making use directly address the challenge of being personally effective.

We need to take responsibility for making sense of our ideas, our proposals, plans, intentions, suggestions. This means shaping them so that they make sense to us and also make sense to others. If they don't, then we need to make sense of others' reactions to our ideas and reshape the ideas so that they make more sense.

We need to mind the gap, the particular circumstances in which we're working. We need to make sense of it. Contexts and people are only ever partially and indirectly within our control, so we need to take responsibility for making sense of these features of our situation and shape them to be receptive to our ideas. If they are not, then *we* need to take the responsibility for making sense of what is happening and for shaping another attempt.

We need to shape our actions so that they make sense, so that they achieve what we intend them to achieve. This means we need to make sense of the effects that they are likely to have and the impacts that they do have. Shaping our actions is our responsibility. It can belong to no one else.

Our ideas. Our gap. Our actions. The idea-action gap.

So what does being personally effective look like?

You are clued up. You are alert to what is going on. You pursue your ideas in the full knowledge that these endeavours will run up against obstacles and pitfalls. You are on the look-out. You pick up clues and reflect on what they might mean.

You can make sense of your context. You are highly aware of the nature of the idea-action gap. You know that there are different ways of making sense of what's going on. You use different angles so that your sense making does justice to the complexity of the situation in which you're working.

You can make sense of your choices. You can see and shape alternatives for action. You can give yourself choices.

You appreciate consequences. You understand the implications of what's going on and you can anticipate the likely consequences of your choices.

You commit yourself. You know that the responsibility for putting your ideas into action is yours. You know that events will move on without you, and are not likely to move in the desired direction without your active intervention.

So where do we go from here?

idea-action gap

clued up

momentum

You may have found this angle a bit unusual. If you were looking for a checklist of advice on what to do, then you may be wondering when we're getting to it.

Bear with us. We will come to that or at least closer to it. But the key point is that you're never going to make effective use of that sort of advice unless you first have a grasp of the particular context in which you are working.

Minding the gap is always a priority. The idea-action gap is the first angle because it is the context for all the rest. If personal effectiveness happens at all, then it takes place in the idea-action gap. This is where it is situated. The angles which follow are sources of clues, ways of looking at the gap, at the choices for action that are open to us, and at some of the consequences of those choices, and therefore serve both to clarify the gap and how to get through it.

an episode on
the idea-action gap

And now, as they say, for something completely different.

Before you read on, we need to let you know that this next bit is unlike any of the others in this book. To start with, it's the first of the episodes, which, as we explained in the introduction, provide a real-life example of the issues covered in our angles. The episodes are less tidy than the angles. Just like real life. The clues are embedded in the story and aren't always obvious. Just like real life. The story is fairly complex and multi-dimensional. Like real life. And, because this is the first episode, we need to take a bit longer to set the scene. This means that there are a couple of pages of introduction and then an extended slab of text, as we let one of the protagonists tell the first part of this business start-up story in his own words.

You might start to wonder where it's all going.

So let's just say a bit more about why we've included the episodes, and then you can decide how you want to handle this one. The purpose of the episodes is to make it easier for you to take development points out of the book and transfer them into practice. The Networker story illustrates many of these points.

So, as always, you have a choice.

If you like case examples, you can follow the Networker story as we've presented it, unfolding between our angles. Alternatively, you could read all the angles first and go back to the early episodes after that if you feel the need for an in-depth illustration. You could even read the case story before the angles if you prefer.

The choice is yours.

But whatever you decide, don't miss the last episode!

It's different again, as you'll see when you get there. (Unless you've already read it!)

Networker

The idea was born, as they often are, in a bar.

Carl and Kim had just got back to England. They hadn't expected to be spending a January afternoon in an English pub. If everything had gone according to plan, they would have been half a world away, somewhere in Asia or India. But their plan, to take a year out to trek round the world, had been cut short by an accident on a South American mountainside. Kim's recuperation became the priority and brought them home to England. Then they were faced with a choice. Return to the United States and pick up their careers as vice presidents in large corporations, or stick with their instinct to seek a change. They opted for change, not surprisingly for two people who got married in a hot air balloon and who skydive for recreation.

Carl applies information technology. It comes easily to him to absorb the intricacies of computing languages and system architectures. He likes assessing business needs and developing innovative, practical solutions to exploit established and emerging technology. He knows what he's doing in this area and his speed of promotion in the corporate hierarchy reflects that.

Kim is one of nature's extroverts. Networking comes easily to her. As she and Carl were thinking through what they might do next, it was her idea that they should talk to Malcolm McNeill.

Malcolm McNeill is director of the Genesis Centre, an independently owned training and development establishment offering its own specially designed programme of 'life skills for the aspiring professional and manager'. The Genesis programme draws from a wide variety of developmental and cultural traditions and includes a combination of individual and group work, both indoor and out. The programme is a lengthy, intensive, demanding experience and for most participants the effect is life-changing. Some go on to change careers. Others return to their previous roles. Almost all consider that they are clearer and more focused about their aims and about themselves as a result of the experience.

Kim knew Malcolm well. Being on the Genesis programme herself had led directly to her going to work in the United States.

Buying a pint for Malcolm, however, hadn't been her first thought. What she had wanted to do was to contact other people who had been on the Genesis programme. They were a diverse group. Networking with them would certainly stimulate ideas, and perhaps open up a number of specific possibilities.

The problem was how to get in touch with them. The Genesis Centre seemed to have no mechanisms for this purpose. So, over a drink, the idea of Networker was born.

Carl's story

The reason we started Networker was to try to bring former participants closer together, where people are really sharing information and helping each other.

We found they tended to cluster in their own stream or sub-group and, after they left Genesis, they wouldn't be in touch with each other or with Malcolm. It seems like they just go out the door and that's it.

So we wanted to see if there was a way we could help them with that.

At that point our idea was something very simple, just a basic way they could share information.

And the idea of Networker sort of grew from there.

When we went to Malcolm, he said, 'I *could* do with this, but what I *really* need at the moment is to be pushing the marketing, I need to be able to make people more aware of Genesis, get more people on the programme, get more placements for people coming off it.'

So we got sidetracked in a way on to developing the Genesis website and that took quite a while to do, about three months. It was very much a learning experience because this wasn't something we'd done previously.

And at that point we were doing the website for free, as a favour.

Once we got that done we said now we need to think about Networker.

We had a lot of ideas while we were developing the website. However the terms had changed slightly. We know this is not a commercial venture in this context. We're not going to make money on it.

So we had to find a way to at least get some money to stay alive on, enough to keep us ticking over while we were developing it. We thought that shouldn't be too hard an issue.

Malcolm said the Genesis Centre's parent organization might have some issues with that. It was used to getting money, it doesn't really spend it.

We also raised the point that the Genesis Association [an association of former participants] ought to be trying to do this sort of thing as well. Malcolm suggested we should speak to them and bring them in.

So we drafted a paper outlining the sort of things we could do and the benefits it could give. One of the things that brought home was that the idea is very hard to explain conceptually. People want to see or feel or understand what it will mean to them: how will it work? How will they interact with it?

idea-action gap

clued up

momentum

So we put together an experience for the first-time user. To take you through the process. To a certain extent. Not the whole thing, but a starting point for talks.

Then Malcolm said he would arrange a meeting with Mattie from the Genesis Association.

Okay, let's just hold Carl there for a moment. Have you picked up any clues yet? Remember what we're trying to illustrate with the episode is the issue of the idea-action gap.

Here are a couple of open-ended questions to help you catch your first impressions. Give them a moment's thought.

◆ What strikes you as significant as you read Carl's story?

◆ What clues have you noticed?

Did you notice how quickly the original idea turned into something else?

Keep watching.

Malcolm hadn't seen our document himself at this point, but he arranged for us all to get together.

Now one of the things Malcolm had stressed right from the start was that the idea must not affect the Genesis Association in any way. He said they were getting a little money from subscriptions, but that wasn't paying its way at the moment and the Association needed this money for its annual reunion conference.

The area they really make money from is in finding companies suitable staff. So they have a recruitment side and provide access to Genesis participants by contacting them directly to see if they're interested in what the companies have to offer. Then they take a placement fee.

That was one thing Malcolm was very clear about. He didn't want us to take any revenue stream away from that. He didn't want Networker to be seen as a threat to that in any way. One thing with Networker was that, because it would enable people to exchange information, they could exchange information about jobs and in that way it could be seen as a threat to the Association. So we drafted the document and we recognized in it that we had to find a way to show that.

We also felt Networker should not be tied to the Association subscription.

A large part of the reason was that the site was not going to be a 'broadcast' medium. Neither the Association nor the Genesis Centre would be putting a lot of information in with the community then consuming that information. It would be much more based on former participants themselves putting the information in.

The Genesis people have the real information, they're the ones out there doing the jobs, pursuing the careers; they know what's what. So newer Genesis people might be posting questions on Networker and older ones would be putting in info saying, 'I've been there, I've done this. Here's what I can tell you.'

That way the new Genesis people would have access to all this information and experience from their relevant career or business sector from the time they started on the programme.

Now the problem with charging for something like that is that the moment you charge a fee you make the fee-payer feel like a consumer, so they say to themselves, 'I'm paying for this service, so why should I be paying to put stuff into it?' We felt that a fee would very much kill the possibility of getting input.

Neither the Centre nor the Association had the spare resources to maintain a wide information base, or create a bigger one, which you'd need to operate as a broadcast medium. So we felt the only option was to make it free to all Genesis participants, whether they went on to join the Association or not.

The other aspect is that if it's only available to subscription payers, then other people who aren't in the Association are not going to appear in the lists, so when you search you'll only get a minority of the contacts, maybe 20 per cent of the total.

Then it becomes a very limited universe, so you don't get much info or sharing and you remove people's wish to share, and these things are critical.

You have to have a certain momentum.

You have to have people continuing to use, otherwise it becomes stale and stagnant and people just don't bother any more.

So that was stressed in our document. It was one of the first things that we said. One of the fundamental principles is that we don't charge.

At the same time we recognized that the Association needed to have some way of generating a revenue stream, so we said we could put *that* inside a 'premium' area, where the Association could generate content and services that people would pay for.

The difference would be that the information coming into Networker would be unproven in many respects, but the Association could offer proven information, from established sources, as part of the service for your subscription. Conversation among Genesis people is for free, but you pay for advice from the Association.

That was one point.

Another was about where information was held. Info about participants on Genesis is held in two separate places at the moment. We felt that if we put this in a combined system in Networker, then participants could maintain it themselves, so that both the Centre and the Association always had the latest information. The onus of keeping it current would shift to the participants and this would free up Association resources.

Another idea was that we could also help the Association by providing a mechanism whereby Genesis participants could submit resumés or indicate that they were interested in being recommended to companies.

We also suggested the idea of discrete advertising. Typically you can earn a penny per display of an advert on a site. The benefit is you have a focused market you can sell to advertisers. Maybe getting a couple of pence doesn't sound a lot, but if each user logs in and looks at ten pages and if they go in once a month, then you start getting reasonable revenue.

We suggested lots of tools and ways of generating revenue and of offsetting the costs they would be incurring for our product.

So this was our proposal.

Time to interrupt Carl's narrative for another reflective moment. Perhaps you're getting impatient. Where is this idea-action gap? Not always obvious. That's the point. Where are the clues? Not always obvious either. More usually embedded. Hints and glimpses. The clues are out there. Okay, one more helping from Carl before we pick them out.

Anyway, Kim and I had the meeting with Malcolm and Mattie. Malcolm prefaced it all. Part of the issue we had was that Malcolm was very aware of the concerns that Mattie might have and he tried to compensate and put her at ease. But unfortunately that had the effect of making her think that there *was* something that she should be worried about.

He hadn't told her much beforehand, so she didn't know exactly what she was coming for. The way he set the scene was very much along the lines of 'Carl and Kim have come up with this idea…there are certain things here that might…I can't remember his exact words…that may change the way the relationship might be between the Centre and the Association…we're trying to do this, that and the other…all things like that.

The effect was that Mattie got more tense rather than less. She couldn't see where the worry was but got worried because he was trying so hard to reassure her.

She skimmed through the document, immediately saw the part about the recruitment side and was concerned about it. From what we could tell from subsequent discussions with her, she very much saw that Networker would do these things and be in conflict with the Association.

Whereas it had been our intention right from the start to make these suggestions simply to enable Networker to help the Association.

So that got off on a bad foot. There was no anger, but throughout that meeting she got more and more tight-lipped and reserved, but she wouldn't say anything. It was sort of just 'Yes – *pause* – okay,' slowly with no expression.

It was fascinating, because even after we explained to her that these premium-area ideas were solely for the Association and if she didn't want to do it she didn't have to do it, obviously it had immediately focused itself in her head that this was something that would threaten the Association or take money from it and we weren't able to dispel that properly at the start.

Which was weird.

So Kim and I went away saying, 'Why wasn't she interested?' We'd expected a very positive reaction, but we didn't really get it.

Malcolm said he thought everything was fine and Mattie went away to discuss it with her board.

Then when she came back, it was basically liking the idea. She said, 'I've been thinking about something like this myself.' She had some concerns about this, that and the other, including the recruitment and various areas. So we then went and spent a whole day with her, just Kim and I, going through it in detail.

At that point I thought we really made a lot of progress. Mattie was very open and honest. She said exactly what her concerns were and her position was. She said she had felt that she'd been brought in halfway through a process, that we sort of conspired together and then brought her in. We dispelled the idea that Malcolm had had the document beforehand and explained that we were being perfectly honest with her.

We had a very full and frank exchange of views, and we came away feeling really positive.

'She's bought into it and can see the benefits.'

She shared some other information with us about the discussions she'd had [with the Association Board] and her being asked, 'Could we get them – Carl and Kim – to do this project with the Association and not the Centre?' But she had responded, 'No, I don't think they will.' So she started being very open with us, behaving very differently to the previous meeting.

We got a complete turnround. We felt at that point that all parties were able to be honest with each other. There was no hidden agenda.

Mattie said, 'This is good, we want to be able to go forward from here and pass all this information around' and there were various exchanges between her and us and Malcolm.

The next stage was to take it to the Genesis Association board.

Mattie is the vice chairman. The chairman is abroad frequently, so Mattie has a lot of control, although she isn't ultimately the lead figure. In any event he wasn't going to be there for this board meeting so that was fine.

Mattie said that when the board members came together it would be a great time to meet them all and to discuss the idea. 'Obviously we need a bit of a meeting beforehand on some other issues, but we're going to have a back room at the Genesis Centre, if you can turn up there about six o'clock.'

So we turned up at that time. We came and we knocked and the door was answered by one of the board members, who simply said 'Yes?' We said, 'We're here for the meeting.' And he said, 'We're not ready for you yet.'

This felt very strange, very negative. Kim instantly felt attacked, but we said, 'Okay, you're not ready for us yet, we'll go away. You'll come and let us know when you're ready.'

But it was concerning. We could see Mattie in the background talking to some other people, but this guy just said, 'We're not ready for you yet.'

So we went back to the bar.

to be continued…

Thinking about it…

Before we offer you our thoughts about Carl's story, we suggest it would be useful for you to collect your own. So here are some more pointed questions. Choose a few to think about.

◆ Did any particular words that Carl used in telling the story leap off the page at you? If so, what struck you about them?

◆ What did you notice about the idea?

◆ How would you describe the gap that Carl and Kim were trying to get their idea across?

◆ How would you describe the context in which they are trying to be personally effective?

- Who else was trying to get an idea across? What happened to their ideas?

- At what points did people have choices to make? And what choices did they make?

- Did they appear to consider other options?

- What were the consequences of the choices they did make?

- Do you think there is much action in this story?

- Where is the action?

A commentary

One of the main themes of this book is that 'the truth is *not* out there'. Working life is not a matter of finding the right answer but of seeing possibilities – possible pitfalls, possible opportunities – and making something of them. So any commentary we offer on Carl's story, and the other episodes in the Networker story, can only be an interpretation. It's a case of having to make some sense of it, using a variety of angles to do that.

So how did Carl and Kim go about making sense of the situation they found themselves in, particularly when their idea encountered the gap? And how did they then go about shaping that situation?

Here are our thoughts.

But before we get into them, a word of preparation. This may feel a bit like one of those school lessons where you have to analyze a piece of text to death. We're doing it at some length here to build up your sensitivity to clues. Because the clues don't linger. After this you'll have to be alert for them yourself.

What struck us as significant as we heard Carl's story?

He tells it very fluently. You've just read it as he told it.

Now the story won't exactly capture all the nuances and uncertainties that Carl experienced at the time, during the moment-by-moment flow of events. That would be too much for him, or for any of us, to remember. We all sort our experience into a shape that makes sense to us. So Carl's story is the record of his experience, and becomes our insight into his understanding of the experience. Carl's story is a great reminder that we're all engaged in an ongoing, constructive process of sense making. That's what we do with our experiences.

There aren't many apparent difficulties.

On the face of it, the idea doesn't seem to be confronting a very difficult gap. Not many people are involved, meetings between them seem to be easy to arrange. There appear to be lots of opportunities in the situation. Carl and Kim seem to have anticipated the obvious problem and have shaped their document to get round it.

What clues did we notice?

Listening to Carl tell his story, we get some benefit from his hindsight because it enables him to stress and accent things that may not have struck him as important until after the event. Yet even so, listening to (or reading) his story for the first time, there is an opportunity to make a mental note of the points that sound as if they *might* turn out to be significant. This is an exercise in catching the clues, in the moment.

◆ The original idea got sidetracked. '*So we got sidetracked in a way on to developing the Genesis website and that took quite a while to do, about three months.*'

◆ The newcomer to the idea is not given much of a pre-briefing. '*He hadn't told her much beforehand, so she didn't know exactly what she was coming for.*'

Did any particular words that Carl used in telling the story leap out at us?

◆ Threat: '*He (Malcolm) didn't want Networker to be seen as a threat.*' Hmm, threat is a strong word.

◆ Skimmed: '*She skimmed through the document.*' Mattie sounds a bit anxious.

- Conspired: '*She had felt…that we sort of conspired together.*' Sounds like a strong reaction.

- Momentum: '*You have to have a certain momentum…otherwise it becomes stale and stagnant.*' This was bound to catch our attention, writing a book for people with momentum.

Clues often come in the form of single words, especially ones that seem strong or come unexpectedly or that echo ideas which are already at the front of our minds.

What did we notice about the idea?

- It takes Carl a long time to explain it. This is not because he is inarticulate. On the contrary. It's because it's a complex idea and a new one, the shape of which is still emerging. '*The idea is very hard to explain conceptually.*' It's hard to get ideas across unless and until we can explain them concisely. '*People want to see or feel or understand what it will mean to them: how will it work?*'

How would we describe the gap that Carl and Kim were trying to get their idea across?

- Let's borrow their own words, because these seem to us to sum it up. '*It was very much a learning experience because this wasn't something we'd done previously.*'

How would we describe the context in which they were trying to be personally effective?

Above all the context is interpersonal. Notice how the idea is developed through a series of interactions between people. First Carl and Kim, then Carl and Kim and Malcolm, then Carl and Kim and Malcolm and Mattie, then Carl and Kim and Mattie. Then '*the next stage was to take it to the Genesis Association board*'. The quality of the interactions between the people involved is going to be a vital feature of the context in which the idea is going to flourish, or not.

Who else was trying to get an idea across? What happened to their ideas?

Although Carl and Kim's Networker is the big idea in this story, we noticed a number of others, three in particular:

◆ Malcolm put across the idea that Networker *must not* be a threat to the Association's revenue stream. This message certainly got across to Carl and Kim because they proceeded to give the idea a lot more thought.

◆ Malcolm also tried to put across the idea to Mattie that Networker *would not* be a threat. However, this time he was much less successful. *'He tried to compensate and put her at ease.'* But unfortunately, as Carl observed, this had exactly the opposite effect to the one Malcolm had intended.

◆ Mattie put an idea across during the first meeting that she attended. *'Throughout that meeting she got more and more tight-lipped and reserved.'* An idea came across. *'Kim and I went away saying, 'Why wasn't she interested?'* That's the idea that came across, but was that the idea that Mattie was trying to convey? *'When she came back, it was basically liking the idea.'*

At what points did people have choices to make? And what choices did they make?

Again there are several, but some that seem to be significant are:

◆ Carl and Kim's decision to stress that Networker should be a free service. *'It was one of the first things that we said. One of the fundamental principles is that we don't charge.'*

◆ Malcolm's decision to arrange the meeting with Mattie before seeing Carl and Kim's document himself. *'Malcolm hadn't seen our document himself at this point, but he arranged for us all to get together.'*

◆ Mattie's decision to say very little during the meeting – *'She wouldn't say anything. It was sort of just 'Yes – pause – okay'* – followed by her subsequent decision to be much more open at the next meeting.

Did they appear to consider other options?

Notice especially the point when Carl says, *'So we felt the only option was to make it free to all.'* Remember the importance of generating alternative courses of action when we find ourselves in a difficult situation. Maybe they did. Maybe *'the only option'* is a loose expression that doesn't do justice to the full range of possibilities that were considered. Maybe. But *'only option'* is a phrase to listen for, a clue that the idea-action gap might be closing in.

Which is not to say that there won't be times when you decide that there is only one option that you're prepared to accept.

Just be aware of, and prepared for, the consequences of that choice.

For the other choices – Malcolm inviting Mattie to the meeting without pre-briefing her, and Mattie's decision to say very little at that meeting – we just don't know whether they considered other options. Perhaps we'll find out later.

What were the consequences of the choices that they did make?

The insistence by Carl and Kim that Networker should be free seems to have been the trigger to Mattie's initial reaction.

The lack of a pre-briefing seems to have put Mattie on guard and threatened to derail the progress of the Networker idea.

Mattie's initial reticence left Carl and Kim feeling blocked and confused. *'Why wasn't she interested? We'd expected a very positive reaction.'* And her subsequent openness left them feeling on the move and optimistic. *'At that point I thought we really made a lot of progress…a very full and frank exchange, and we came away feeling really positive.'*

Do we think there is much action in this story?

Oh yes. There's a lot going on here even if it is not particularly obvious or dramatic.

Where is the action?

'Obviously it had immediately focused itself in her head that this was something that would threaten the Association or take money from it and we weren't able to dispel that.'

idea-action gap

clued up

momentum

'Malcolm said he thought everything was fine.'

We said, 'We're here for the meeting.' And he said, 'We're not ready for you yet.' This felt very strange, very negative. Kim instantly felt attacked.

The action is in the apparently small stuff, in what people say – in the words they choose, or don't take much care to choose, to express themselves; in the thoughts and feelings that occur to them when they first hear something. The action is in the moment.

Working in the moment.

Messy, isn't it?

The clues are embedded in the flow of events.

They don't immediately make sense. We have to make sense of them and we have to do it progressively. More importantly, we don't have to wait until after the event to do it. We can, and need to, gather clues as we go along. We need as rich a harvest of clues as we can gather for the sense making that we need to get to grips with the context in which we're working. We need to be actively, attentively thinking as we go along.

But that's not easy. As we noted earlier, our stock of attention is limited and often it's exactly when we need it most, in difficult or complex situations, that it is already most committed and we have the least available for catching and making sense of those elusive, in-the-moment clues.

So how do we manage our attention and our thinking? That is the subject of our next angle.

good thinking

an angle on
good thinking
making the most of what's already there

Is your thinking good? How can you tell? Think about your thinking for a moment. Not about your thoughts, but about your thinking. How would you describe it? These are tough questions, but important ones if we want to get our ideas into action. So what answers did you come up with?

Certainly we all like to think that our thinking is pretty good. But how do we tell?

And how much *do* we think about our thinking? Not often. Not often enough, as this chapter is going to suggest. And when we do make the effort to think about our thinking, what happens? We find that it's difficult to do. It's hard to find words to describe our thinking, because when we try, we just seem to come back to our thoughts. And thoughts are usually the product of our thinking rather than the thinking itself. We're up against a black box. We can see the outputs, but it's hard to see the process that creates and shapes them.

The way we think – its character, its quality – tend to be invisible. And this is hardly surprising because for the most part our thinking is automatic. It's a process that runs in the background, leaving the front of our minds free to concentrate on other things, like who just joined the meeting and the content of what they're saying, and how other people are reacting to that, and what we might think about it ourselves. There's usually more than enough clamouring for our mind's attention.

So why should we give some of that attention to the character of our own thinking? Why does it matter?

The short answer is that it matters precisely because there is so much in modern occupational life competing for our attention: material to read and understand, meetings to prepare for and attend, problems to identify and solve, plans to make and implement, relationships to establish and develop, questions to ask and answer. The list goes on. Confronted with this barrage of mental demands, we hit mental overload. And when we hit that overload, the quality of our thinking goes down, and drags our personal effectiveness with it.

Built for speed

Speed is generally a source of competitive advantage. That's certainly true for cars and other forms of transport, for computers and communication systems, and for businesses seeking to bring their products and services to market. So it's not surprising to find that the human mind is basically built for speed.

Think about it. We're in animated conversation with someone. We hear what they say and respond promptly. They hear us and come straight out with a reply. Typically the gaps – if any – are short. The mental processing involved is fast. Take another situation. We're travelling from a strange airport. Even though we've never been there before, we know the sorts of things to look for: the check-in desk, the departures board, the security screening. We have a script for this sort of occasion, so we don't need to think too hard about it. We know the sorts of clues to look for and an approximate clue is

good thinking

clued up

momentum

enough to guide our actions. At the risk of torturing the metaphor, we're on automatic pilot. We don't need to think deeply or even particularly carefully because we recognize what's going on and we can take the appropriate actions apparently without thinking. Think about how often you've locked your front door or your car and then wondered, as you've walked away, whether you have remembered to do so.

For the most part, this is a good thing. If we had to put a lot of thinking into every activity, we would not get much done. The fact that so much of our everyday thinking can be, and is, done automatically and unconsciously leaves us with mental resources available to invest conscious attention into more demanding mental challenges. This is efficient.

So, to go back to our earlier question, what can we say about our thinking? We can say that it tends to be fast, it's often spontaneous rather than considered, it relies heavily on recognizing and following patterns, and that it doesn't demand – or receive – much in the way of conscious attention. It is a pattern that has been described by Harvard's David Perkins as 'default thinking': 'hasty, narrow, fuzzy and sprawling.'

Why such harsh words? What's the problem with default thinking?

We're back, as we were with the concept of the idea-action gap, to the problem of context.

The problem of context

Default thinking is fine when we're dealing with something familiar or routine or where the consequences of a poor decision are insignificant. But default thinking is a problem when we're dealing with something novel or unfamiliar, or where the risks are high and the potential consequences of a poor decision are great. Occupational life these days is full of such high-stake situations.

Consider some examples:

- Delivering an important presentation and handling a searching question-and-answer session.

- Responding to an unexpected request from a client or other stakeholder.

- Negotiating a deal.

- Considering the offer of a new job.

- Starting up a new business venture.

- Having to give feedback to someone, especially when that person is a peer or a boss rather than someone who works for you.

- Planning a project implementation.

- Tackling a complex problem.

Some of these examples are comparatively infrequent occurrences. Others are everyday events. The occasions when default thinking can get us into trouble are perhaps more common than we realize.

But I know how to brainstorm!

Is the picture as bleak as we are suggesting? A first reaction is often to protest. *'You're exaggerating. When we need to think carefully, we have techniques. We use SWOT analysis, and the problem-solving wheel, and…and that thinking hats thing and…brainstorming. Yes, we're always using brainstorming!'* The difficulty is not that good techniques do not exist. The central difficulty is that we tend not to use the means of good thinking that do exist.

This is partly because the habit of default thinking is very strong. It is also because there are so many thinking tools and techniques to remember.

As we pointed out when we were looking at the idea-action gap, one of the major problems with being personally effective is that there is an embarrassment of good advice on the subject. We are overloaded with it. And we know what happens to our thinking when we're overloaded.

What we need is a repertoire of approaches to good thinking that's small enough that we can carry it easily in our heads, yet at the same time powerful enough to give us good thinking capabilities to meet the wide range of thinking challenges that we must expect to encounter. We need a distinctive brand of thinking.

GOOD – a distinctive brand of thinking

G   is for give thinking time.

O   is for open it.

O   is for organize it.

D   is for deepen it.

Good thinking is the antidote to default thinking. Each of the elements of good thinking tackles one of the shortcomings of default thinking. GOOD isn't the world's greatest acronym, but it does point us towards a set of habits for superior thinking.

Give thinking time

The most basic failure in our thinking tends to be that we simply don't give it enough time. Time, of course, is *the* scarce commodity these days, reflected in new catch-phrases like 'time famine'. Organizational and occupational life is busier than ever before. *'Some hope!'* you might then exclaim when we say that you need to give thinking time. There are plenty of other claims on your time already waiting in the queue.

But this is the paradox. Giving time makes time. Giving time to thinking makes our subsequent actions more effective. Giving time to sense making enables us to understand the gap that we are facing and to shape our ideas and actions more appropriately.

Is it difficult to give thinking time? The instinctive answer is, yes.

But that's default thinking kicking in again. Let's pose the question another way. What makes it difficult to give thinking time? The pressure to get things done. But that's a feature of our modern working environment, part of its messiness. That comes with the territory. More importantly, *who* makes it difficult to give thinking time?

We do.

Try this little thought experiment. What does someone look like when they're thinking? The picture usually conjured up by that question is of someone sitting still, passive, unmoving, like Rodin's statue of *The Thinker*, head on hand. But does this mean that nothing is happening? No.

We make it difficult to give thinking time because we forget that thinking is an integral part of action. We forget that behaving without thinking is simply reflex, or instinct, not action, not shaping.

So how do we give time to thinking? For a start, by recognizing it as part of action. By recognizing thinking as one of the most important actions that we ever have to take. We need to drop the false dichotomy that sees thinking and action as opposites. They're not. Someone Alan was coaching recently came up with a marvellous expression for this when she said, *'I hadn't realized until now, but thinking is so…energetic!'*

She had discovered a new-found respect for thinking. She was giving it respect in the best way we can, by giving it a share of our most precious and irreplaceable resource, our time.

At a very practical level, the way to give time to thinking is very simple. It is by interrupting whatever else we are doing. We do this as a matter of course for people or events that we like or value. We will interrupt what we are doing to pay attention to them. It's simply a case of doing the same for thinking. And the great thing is that a little bit of time invested in thinking can yield a disproportionate return. Because our default tendency is to be hasty, even a few minutes of organized thinking action can make a big difference.

It's not just okay to take time out for thinking. It's essential. In the flow of questioning, when you're stuck for an answer, or you feel your answering wandering off the point, stop. Collect your thoughts. In the midst of discussing an issue, especially when the discussion doesn't seem to be making any progress, don't just keep talking. Stop. Focus on a question. Take time to think about it. Take two or three minutes. It's not long in the great scheme of things and it will contribute far more than it takes. Give thinking time.

Open your thinking

Good thinking is not just about how much thinking we do. It's not just about quantity. The quality is also important and the first ingredient of quality thinking is for it to be open.

What do we mean by open? Again, the contrast is with one of the shortcomings of default thinking, in this case its tendency to be narrow. Default thinking sees what it expects to see, which is not necessarily what is actually there. Go back for a moment to the sorts of hostile environment that we were considering in our first angle. Default thinking in the jungle might see a rough-barked log offering a convenient way of keeping your feet out of the water. Good thinking might recognize that same rough texture as a half-submerged crocodile. Good thinking would certainly recognize that as a possibility.

That is one of the hallmarks of good thinking – it is open to possibilities. It does not leap to conclusions in situations where the evidence is unclear or the risks of a mistake are high. Good thinking is on the look-out for alternatives. Good thinking is an explorer first and foremost. As Edward de Bono, originator of the term 'lateral thinking', points out in his many books on the improvement of thinking, one of our most common failings is to judge prematurely, without adequate exploration of possibilities.

Being open in our thinking is not a question of technique. It is a matter of mindset.

We don't actually need a toolkit of problem-solving methods or have to remember an array of step-by-step procedures to be open in our thinking. We simply need to approach things in an open-minded way. It's a matter of disposition.

Here's another word that encapsulates what we mean by open thinking, 'mindfulness'. (New words can help our thinking. One of the things that handicaps our ability to think about our thinking is that we don't have a rich enough vocabulary to describe it or to distinguish between the characteristics of good and bad thinking.) *'Mindfulness.'* This is a word coined by Harvard Professor of Psychology Ellen Langer which she uses as a contrast with the mindlessness that characterizes so much thinking.

She sees three principal features in a mindful approach. First, openness to new information. This is what we think of as an alertness for clues, receptiveness, a readiness to take in new data without prejudging their significance or screening them out because they don't immediately seem to fit our expectations.

Second, mindfulness is open to multiple perspectives rather than having only one frame of reference to guide our actions. In terms of being clued up this means having and using a variety of angles, understanding how each works, what sorts of choices they offer and what the likely implications of these choices will be.

Third, mindfulness involves the continuous creation of categories. In our terms, this means not just fitting clues into their obvious slots but actively looking for new and unobvious ways of making sense of them, new and unobvious ways of shaping our course of action. In other words, creating new meanings and choices.

So good thinking is open. It is broad in its range of inputs, open to the possible meaning of those inputs, and adventurous in how it uses them.

clued up

momentum

Organize your thinking

The previous section makes good thinking sound like something of a buccaneer, a free-spirit answerable to none. But that does not do it justice. Nor buccaneers for that matter, for they too had rules and organization. As good thinking must. Good thinking is organized.

Default thinking on the other hand is prone to sprawl, to shapelessness.

Cast your mind back to doing exams that involved writing essays. Remember the difference between writing one where your plan was clear and structured and one where you had struggled, or perhaps simply omitted, to create a plan. Remember how that experience felt as the clock raced round and the words crawled slowly on to the page?

So how do we organize our thinking?

Giving it time is an essential ingredient, but it's not the whole story. We've probably all sat staring vacantly at a blank page or a computer screen, trying to get our thoughts organized but finding it difficult to get going. Here are three ways of going about it, progressing from a broad-brush approach to a more refined one.

In or out?

Ask yourself, 'What am I trying *to do* with my thinking here?' At the most general level, we have the choice of taking our thinking in one of only two directions: out or in. Do we need it to diverge or converge? If our thinking seems to be stuck on one particular point or issue and is simply going round in circles, then it's time to diverge. We need to broaden our thinking, generate more options, explore more possibilities. If our thinking seems to be overwhelmed with the variety of ideas and issues, then it's time to narrow it down. In that case we need to use converging devices, such as prioritizing, applying explicit criteria, rank ordering, and other forms of forced choice.

Step-wise

An alternative approach to organizing our thinking is to design a process for it. Tools such as the problem-solving wheel are essentially of this sort, step-by-step approaches to guide the application of our thinking and other forms of action. But there is no necessity to feel compelled to follow these tools slavishly. In our experience it is often the case that even when people remember that such tools exist, they don't use them because they worry that they cannot recall them accurately or use them *properly*.

That's an inhibition we can cheerfully lose.

In a practical world which is primarily interested in effective answers, we don't need to get hung up about 'right' answers.

We shouldn't be in thrall to the theory. We can devise our own processes. And we should, because a step-by-step process is essentially a strategy for dealing with a challenge. And there are plenty of challenges out there.

So we can organize our thinking by devising little step-by-step processes for it. For example, I have to run a meeting this afternoon and I need to think about it beforehand. I take a piece of paper and sketch out a design for the meeting. It doesn't take long and it looks like this:

good thinking

clued up

momentum

> **Group feedback meeting**
>
> 1. Introduction: purpose & process
> 2. In turn, each participant introduces own learning objectives (briefly)
> 3. All prepare feedback on each other (privately, using sticky notes)
> 4. Post feedback to each other
> 5. Individuals read inputs (privately)

But hang on! That didn't take long. And I'm getting a clue. It's coming from the voice inside my head that's saying, 'It's not going to be that easy.' This is a clue that I need to think about my thinking, give it some more time, open it up, make it deeper. So I need to organize my thinking.

Okay, I'm going to start by giving myself five minutes to come up with an organizer for my thinking on this one.

And here's what I came up with.

> **Thinking about the group feedback meeting**
>
> 1. Collect my thoughts about previous events like this:
>   - my thoughts
>   - other participants
>   - other facilitators
>
> 2. Anticipate the experience
>   - as a participant
>   - how is it likely to feel?
>   - what look like the hot spots?
>   - what unintended impacts might there be?
>   - process for handling concerns

How do the results compare?

They are both processes. But the first is the product of thinking and default thinking at that; the second is the product of thinking about thinking, good thinking. The first organizes the proposed action of the meeting. The second organizes the thinking about the design of the meeting. The first is likely to get me into difficulty. The second is likely to keep me out of it.

Notice also that the second doesn't do all the thinking for me. I still need to do that, especially on points such as *how is it likely to feel* and *process for handling concerns*. It doesn't do the thinking, but it does organize the thinking that needs to be done.

And it only took five minutes.

Give thinking time. It doesn't need a big investment to get a good return.

Frameworks as organizers

A third way of organizing our thinking is by applying a particular frame of reference and using that to provide structure and boundaries for our thinking.

The difficulty in practice is that very often our frames of reference are neither clear nor explicit. Instead they tend to be unconscious and fuzzy and consequently perpetuate default rather than good thinking.

Frames of reference can be established at many different levels. At a highly encompassing level, the scientific approach, with its emphasis on objectively observed, replicable data, on economy of explanation and on the disproof of alternatives, can be regarded as a frame of reference. At the other extreme, specific tools, such as SWOT (strengths, weaknesses, opportunities and threats) analysis – and the many other analytical organizers that can be formed by plotting a couple of variables in a matrix arrangement – are also frames of reference. The learning cycle that we looked at in the previous chapter is another example of a frame of reference.

The point is that there is no absolutely right or wrong level for a frame of reference.

It is a question of usefulness rather than correctness. Which is at least part of the reason why there are so many frames of reference to choose from.

So we find ourselves back at that recurring problem for personal effectiveness. There are just so many organizers out there. How do we choose?

Here's a radical proposition. Basically it doesn't matter.

It doesn't matter which organizer we choose. What matters is that we use one, so that we can get our thinking moving and follow the train of thought. The alternative is that our thinking drifts and wanders and becomes hard even for us to follow (far less anyone else). Disorganized thinking wastes time and is difficult to manage.

A lot of our work involves listening to other people to arrive at an understanding of what they're trying to achieve and the difficulties they're having en route. Having listened to what they're saying for a while, we'll often collect our thoughts about it around some familiar framework or another: a model of how teams work or how people handle disagreements or of different styles of management, for example. This can be a really helpful way of making sense of someone's experience (including your own) and it can also help you to point out the likely implications of particular patterns of behaviour, and to suggest the alternatives available.

The important thing when using any framework or model or concept as an organizer is to recognize what we're doing. We're coming at the issue from a particular angle. If we don't recognize that, the organizer can easily become a trap which will ultimately constrain rather than improve our thinking. So we're back to our theme: we need to be thinking about our thinking.

So choose an organizer and get started. If that particular organizer doesn't help much, then that in itself is going to be informative. It'll tell us that this isn't a particularly useful way of looking at this particular case. Then we know we need to create another organizer. That's okay. It's important not to get locked into one frame of thinking. And although the quality movement enjoins us to 'get it right first time', that simply isn't very realistic in a messy world. What's more important is to bring some thoughtful organization – and some organization of our thoughts – to the challenge of that messiness.

Deepen your thinking

The reason we can be so liberal in our choice of organizer is that the organization of our thinking is not an end in itself but a means to an end. What's important is not the tidiness of our thinking as such but that our thinking should give us a thorough and useful understanding. Organized thinking helps to do that. Disorganized thinking doesn't. But the real goal is comprehension that we can use in practice. So good thinking requires depth of understanding.

How do we make our thinking deep?

Well, the first point to make is that deep does not mean narrow. We dealt with that particular disadvantage of default thinking earlier. And the next point is that deep does not mean obscure, even though the expression 'That's deep!' often seems to be used as a polite way of saying, 'I don't understand what you're saying!'

What we mean by deep is sound or coherent. Deep thinking produces reliable explanations, ones that we can trust to predict how things will work.

And we'd all like that.

But here's a conundrum. As we've said already (and will continue to emphasize throughout this book), it's a messy world that we have to live and work in. It's not as predictable as we might like it to be. So deep thinking starts to sound like the sort of thing that's okay for scientists and academics to pursue, but frankly not very realistic or relevant for people in the world of business or management.

And that's where we'd be guilty of shallow thinking.

Sure, it's a messy looking world.

It's certainly a complex world, even within the comparatively narrow confines of one particular job: there's a lot going on and things don't stand still. (We'll have more to say about that when we look at complexity in more detail in the next angle.) But that's exactly what makes deep thinking both necessary and difficult.

It's necessary because, as we've seen already, we need to know our way around. To be personally effective, we need to understand how things happen and why. We can usually see the effects (though we're not even as good at that as we might be), but can we see the causes that lie behind them? Remember what we said about the human brain being built for speed. In the same vein, we are prone to think in terms of over-simplistic patterns of cause and effect. We tend to overlook the possibility of multiple causes and multiple effects and repercussions. We tend to see the obvious explanation and stop at that, rather than seeking out the less obvious but more powerful explanations.

We know a photograph that gives a wonderful, simple illustration of this. It shows a policeman running down the street after a spiky-haired, ripped-jeans punk rocker. Both are at full stretch. What's the story? The great majority of people who see this picture go for the obvious explanation. The scruffy-looking one is a criminal and the policeman is chasing him. But the real story is that both of them are chasing the criminal, who is outside the frame of the photograph. An unobvious explanation.

'Well, in real life we'd see that,' you might say. But in occupational life the stories are much more complicated, and ongoing, and the reasons are generally much harder to see. 'Attitude' is a word we'd like to call your attention to as a clue. It's a great clue that deep understanding is missing. *'She seems to have a bit of an attitude problem.'* What does that mean? Usually it means we just don't know why she's behaving as she is. It means we need a deeper explanation.

Let's assume we've made the case for deep thinking in occupational life. It sounds as if we're saying, you have to find the right answer. Not exactly. As we've already said, the occupational and organizational domain is a world of probabilities and possibilities rather than one of certainties. So it doesn't make sense to expect, or spend too much time looking for, the right answer.

But we do need a reasonable answer, a realistic answer.

There are a number of practical things we can do. For a start, we can resist the temptation to seize on the first, or obvious, explanation. It might be the best we can come up with, but before we decide we should think-test it out. Can you think of alternative explanations? A useful approach is to make yourself dream up at least two alternative explanations, however far out they might seem at first. At least this pushes your thinking deeper.

Second, compare and contrast your explanations. This is a good way of exposing the assumptions and the logic – if any – behind them. It makes your thinking deeper by making it more careful.

Then you can expose your explanation to a more severe test. Try out your explanation on someone else, or ideally a number of other people, but do it individually so that you get the full value of their independent views. They'll soon tell you if it sounds plausible or not. For another thing, this will oblige you to express your explanation clearly. It's a good clue that your thinking isn't deep enough if other people can't understand what you're trying to say.

Finally, stay open to other possible explanations. Pay attention, as events unfold, to information which might cause you to revise and refine your explanation. Explanations are not simply presented to us. We have to construct them. And that takes time. So keep your thinking open, and organized, and…

The nature of good thinking

You'll probably have noticed something from that last paragraph. After all, there were some clues at the end of it. When we think about one aspect of good thinking, we often come back to other aspects of it. In considering deep thinking, we find ourselves drawn to the need for open thinking and organized thinking. This interconnectedness points to an important feature of good thinking.

Good thinking is not a rigid procedure. It is not a sequence of steps to be followed.

It is more in the nature of an approach, a set of characteristics to be drawn upon, flexibly, as we work our way through a thinking challenge.

In technical terms (here's a nugget to add to your quiz repertoire) good thinking is a matter of heuristics rather than algorithms. An algorithm is a series of prescribed steps that are guaranteed to lead to the required answer. Heuristics are more like rules of thumb. They will take you in the right direction, improve the odds, but won't in themselves guarantee a right answer.

In a probabilistic world, that seems like the best we can hope to have.

Where our angles fit

We need to think about our thinking. We need to give it time, open it up so that it ranges broadly, organize it so that it proceeds efficiently, and give it depth so that it provides us with realistic explanations of how things happen.

As we've already seen, frameworks are helpful for organizing our thinking. And as we've just noted, one aspect of good thinking tends to relate to another. So it won't come as a surprise to find that frameworks can also help to open up our thinking and to give it depth. They open it up by spelling out at least some of the factors involved. They give it depth by providing an explanation of how these factors relate to one another.

It's good to have a repertoire and our advice is to continue to extend your repertoire. Frames don't guarantee to bring you to the answer.

No frame can do that. All they can do is improve the odds. So load the odds in your favour by having multiple frames of reference.

Which is where our angles come in. They are frameworks too. As frames go, they're looser rather than tighter, but you would expect that by now, given what we've been saying about the dynamic nature of the context we have to work in and the corresponding nature of the thinking that we need to do.

We're offering five angles in this book to extend your repertoire. We've chosen the five that we believe offer the greatest leverage for being personally effective in the context of modern occupational life.

But remember…

◆ Don't get trapped in a single angle.

◆ Don't assume that any particular angle is the only way of thinking.

◆ Don't allow any one angle to become the only guide to your doing.

Think about your thinking. That's where effective action starts.

good thinking

clued up

momentum

an episode on
good thinking

Back to Genesis. Remember Mattie, vice chairman of the Genesis Association. While she runs her own consultancy business, she is also a teacher and mentor on the Genesis programme on which she herself was a participant some years ago. Remember how she was first introduced to the idea of Networker. Here's how the experience felt from her point of view.

Mattie's story

I first became aware something was going on about this time last year, that websites were being created for the Genesis Centre and for the programme. I didn't know who was behind them. They spoke to me as if I knew who was behind it and me being me I didn't really ask too many questions because I felt I wasn't supposed to know because Malcolm hadn't told me.

Jenny, one of the managers at the Centre, mentioned someone called Carl once or twice, then it became apparent that Carl was Kim's partner and things started to fall into place a little more.

A couple of months later Malcolm called me to his office and he was a bit nervous – well that's how I interpret it – and he said, 'We're thinking of doing an interactive website for the Genesis people. I need a vehicle for the foundation programme.'

We had talked about all these ideas for some time, so it wasn't an idea that was foreign to me. But he said, 'We can see this has ramifications for external purposes, for the alumni body.' Now this isn't his territory because it belongs to the Association rather than the Genesis Centre. It's a separate legal entity.

There was a time when the alumni committee ran out of the Centre but a previous director withdrew that support, so I don't think Malcolm is necessarily very comfortable with it.

So he said to me, 'We've got this thing, it's possibly going to impinge on how the Association works. There are all sorts of issues like whether people pay subscriptions.'

I said maybe it could, but I didn't say much because I was trying to pick up as much body language as I could.

He said, 'I'd like you to come to a meeting where Kim and Carl are going to put forward a proposal about this.'

So I went to the meeting.

You make the assumption that everybody else in the room knows all about it, and I felt like the mushroom and I was frightened underneath.

I sat and listened. When I'm like that I sit and listen and I try to read the signs.

Jenny didn't seem her normal self. She seemed a bit tense. I thought, what's going on here? What I didn't know was that she'd been called in at the last minute and didn't know anything about the meeting either.

So we got this enormous document, the Networker discussion paper. I wasn't allowed to disclose this to anybody. I was told it was because this was very leading edge. So I said, 'Okay, let's do this first and then I'll tell you if I can move forward or not, but I can't sell an idea if I'm not allowed to talk about it.'

The paper talks about the service will be available at no charge, that was the very first principle. The objective was the creation of an online community, so there we were, with all these different things it could do.

This is a really well thought-out document. I don't agree with all of it but I was excited about it. I could see a way forward. I said to them, 'You've saved me a lot of work' because I could see this as a good vehicle for selling this to the Association board who can be a bit traditional; a fast-track way of selling a raft of ideas.

But I didn't say all of that at that meeting. It was going through my mind.

I was listening like mad.

I said, 'There's no way I can get the board interested if you don't let me let them see the document.'

I got home and got a letter that talked about all the websites, including the intention to develop Networker, and I thought, 'That load of bastards sat at that meeting knowing what they knew about this document during that meeting, the double-crossing conniving…

Was I wrong to think that? I don't know. I'd had a long drive, I was tired, I'd been down to the meeting on a voluntary basis.

I thought, that's just typical, they can't be open for five minutes.

It just reinforced all the paradigms I already had.

Next morning I rang Jenny. I was very calm. I said, 'How do you think I feel? It seems like a deliberate attempt to wrong-foot the Association.'

I think Jenny hadn't even thought about it. I don't think it had crossed her mind how it would look.

I didn't fall out with her at all. Or with the others. I guess I decided maybe it was an accident.

So I circulated the board and what could they say but 'Yes, we'll have a look at it'? So we made a plan that I'd see Kim and Carl in the office and then they could make a presentation at our next board meeting.

Kim and Carl came and they appeared, and I think it was quite genuine, to be horrified at how the idea had been sold to me and horrified at the effect the letter had had. Kim said, 'I didn't realize how terrible it would seem.'

While they were with us we bought a couple of website names. We paid for them but Kim went in and did it.

Let's hold Mattie's story there for a moment. Now we've seen the start of the Networker project both from Carl and Kim's point of view and from Mattie's. An unexpectedly wobbly take-off, wouldn't you agree? But that's the idea-action gap for you, full of confusion, misunderstandings, unintentional impacts and unintended consequences. A place where each of us makes our own interpretation of what's going on, but with no guarantee that others will form similar views.

So then what happened? Mattie, back to you…

Anyway, the arrangement was that we would have our board meeting and at the appointed moment Kim and Carl would knock on the door, come in and make a presentation. They came perhaps a bit early or we were a bit late, but Kim said, 'May we come in?' and before any of us could say, 'Can you give us five minutes?' Finn, who was sat beside me, said, 'Not at the moment, we're not ready.'

It was quite clear that this was invading his territory.

Finn had done a lot of work in setting up our old website. He'd done it for free. He didn't ask for any money. So I got the feeling that he was not going to be easily sold.

So we asked them to give us ten minutes to get tidied up. Then I took a back seat because I'd been through all this and they didn't need to sell it to me.

The meeting went on for two hours at least, all sorts of questions and exchange, but I think what we agreed to do was meet the following night and bring Malcolm into the discussion and discuss this Networker business, because essentially we all wanted to do it.

Though Finn had reservations. I know because he bristled. He gets quite sharp. It's so difficult to describe. It's the way he asks the question, abrupt. And he and Kim started to tussle even then.

So the next night what was agreed was that we'd look at Networker. There'd be a charge for it. We, the Association, were happy for there to be a price tag to create this thing and a figure was mentioned. That was fine, but there was also going to be an element for the internal bit – the tutors' network – which would mean a relatively small charge to the Genesis Centre and Malcolm said quite openly, 'That's not going to be easy.'

What also came out of that meeting was that we formed a steering group – Kim and Carl, myself, Finn, Malcolm and Saheena. Everybody was happy with that.

Before and after dinner there were lots of little side meetings going on, all sorts of huddles, Kim and Carl in lots of them, obviously doing some backselling. I'm not sure why. I didn't see the need.

We swapped e-mail addresses. It was all going to be done electronically.

I said there was no way I was going to mess around doing it any other way.

I thought that Finn's fears had been 90 per cent alleviated. I'd been watching him.

We agreed that Kim and Carl would produce an outline functional specification in ten weeks' time and then we'd have a meeting, after that had been circulated, and we'd cross the ts and decide to go ahead.

Press the pause button again. So the Networker project collaboration between the Genesis Centre, the Genesis Association and Carl and Kim is up and running. There have been a few tremors underfoot in that old idea-action gap, but nothing seismic, and now the show's on the road.

Or is it?

What have you noticed?

Any clues?

Something is about to change and it becomes apparent in the way Mattie recounts the experience. At this point in the interview she produced a file of papers, several inches thick, placed it on the table in front of her and proceeded to trace the details of the story with reference to it.

See what happens…

Various discussion papers now start circulating. And individual questions from Kim to me. Not once a week, we're getting seven of these a day. And it's not long before we're buckling under the weight of the e-mails. I had to ask her to stop bombarding my assistant with requests for information.

Most of the decisions were being taken between the steering group, but there were odd things that Kim was circulating to the wider group (the whole board) as well, for example this one on funds generation. They had an idea that we could generate money via Amazon book reviews, for example.

There are lots of papers and questions circulating. There's a lot going on.

Then about two weeks after the launch, there's a paper from Carl and Kim, 'An Introduction to Networker', to explain how the specification is emerging and enable them to confirm that they are 'heading down the right route'.

One Wednesday we start getting some very nasty e-mails. We suddenly get this horrible storm erupting, to do with the security of Networker.

This was the huge black cloud in Finn's head, because Networker was an encompassing site, not only accessed by users but also by staff in the Association's office, in the Genesis Centre, possibly by lecturers from remote locations, we didn't know.

What was the shape of this thing? This is what worried him.

I can't get entirely into his mindset, but he definitely had a bee in his bonnet and he went for Kim's jugular.

I couldn't believe it. I'm still trying to work out where all the nastiness came from.

I think it was from a document that Kim circulated to the sub-committee.

I thought it was okay, but Finn came back saying that if the system was providing a service to Genesis people, then it must be trusted by them. He saw it as a question of the security of personal data.

He was really concerned about the web service provider. He felt we needed a formal contract with them and with Kim and Carl before they started building the system. Plus procedures for security and access and what would happen if these were breached.

In his view security was the foundation block to the project and had to precede any other criteria. And he circulated this view to the sub-committee.

The next day there was an e-mail from Carl responding with a security discussion paper, a long, detailed, direct response, trying to address Finn's concerns.

Then very shortly after that – for some reason these things were all being written at three o'clock and six o'clock in the morning – there was another one from Finn to Carl, saying he'd read Carl's proposals with interest but without reaching any conclusions, so Finn posed another series of questions and asked for contributions from the rest of the team.

I couldn't follow this. I began to lose the thread, to wonder what was really bugging him. I couldn't understand some of his comments, like asking whether security was an issue at all – having said all he'd said, that question just didn't make sense to me.

That seemed very odd.

Then that evening there was a paper that wasn't on any of that. It was from Kim, asking for feedback and input on categories of content for the website, but funnily enough she hadn't sent it to the steering group but to the wider board, which struck me as odd.

Then there was one from Finn, asking her to clarify, before he looked at her categories in detail, how she intended to set up the spreadsheet or something. I didn't find this note very easy to understand but the issue they were talking about seemed to be perfectly straightforward.

And there was one from Finn to all of us about Networker relationships, saying that we'd been dealing with grey areas in the nature of the community structure and asking everyone to respond, even though some of the issues might be uncomfortable to deal with.

He said that Networker was an exciting development, but he saw potential threats, that personal data was open to abuse, that it was necessary to minimize the damage from mistakes or rogue individuals and protect the database from unintentional or intentional misuses.

He stressed the need to alleviate as much of this as possible and wanted to know what the board proposed to do with the concerns he'd highlighted.

We're definitely getting towards the bonfire now.

Then there's one from Kim to him. It's on the Friday, though there might have been another in between. It's difficult to follow.

She reminds him that we'd agreed there was a need for things to be written clearly and unambiguously. Then she goes on to say that this includes using punctuation, paragraphs and sections. So we're starting to fight about these e-mails. Then she asks him please to resend his e-mail with the key points broken out, so she can stand a chance of understanding.

This is Kim getting very shirt-baggy with Finn.

She's put that on top of one from him to her earlier in the day, identifying areas that concerned him and saying, 'We have to develop trust to work together' and 'I would appreciate you rewording your paragraph to reflect brevity and clarity'.

Something's happened off-screen here. I think there have been telephone calls too.

Anyway I got on the phone and said, 'Will you two stop doing this.'

I got them both ranting at me. I just had to try to be the broker in the middle.

Let's hold Mattie's story for a while.

What's happening? It doesn't come out from the printed page as clearly as it did in our interview, but between the first excerpt we've given you and the second there is a dramatic change of pace in the way she tells the story. In the first she spoke fluently, few pauses or hesitations. In the second there are long gaps as she slowly reconstructs the sequence of events, referring to her mountainous file of e-mails.

So what's going on? Well, for one thing, she's taking care to be accurate. Working through the documents one at a time, methodically, trying to clarify the flow of events. But it's not easy. Because there's so much of it. And because the documented record is incomplete, as Mattie herself is the first to acknowledge. She prefers not to run off paper copies of e-mail unless she feels she has to. In addition there have been telephone calls leaving no record except perhaps an occasional written file note.

Another difficulty is that Mattie is now describing events in which she was involved indirectly rather than directly. In the first excerpt she's talking about her own first-hand experience. In the second she's describing — and having to make sense of — other people's interactions. Which is altogether harder to do.

A case of complexity

Mattie's account becomes more fragmented. And that's not surprising since that — as she explains to us — is how it felt at the time. '*It's difficult to follow.*' It's an example of having to deal with complexity, a subject that we will be looking at in more detail in our next angle. But in the meantime, this complexity is what Mattie — and the rest of the cast of characters in our everyday occupational drama — are having to deal with.

They all have ideas that they are trying to get across some sort of idea-action gap.

Think about it.

We already know something about the idea that Carl and Kim are trying to turn into action. And now we know something about the idea that Mattie is pursuing. But what is Finn's idea? He's trying to get something across, but what is it? Are we clear about that? Is anyone else? Is he?

We've already seen that a lack of clarity is one of the features of the idea-action gap, but here's another feature. It's multi-faceted. Different people, even when they're working together on the same project, have different ideas that they're trying to get across. Maybe just slightly different ideas, maybe very different. And this is going on all the time. Just to add to the difficulty of making sense of things.

But we've suggested in our last angle that good thinking is a way out of this. So let's look at the quality of our characters' thinking. How are they doing?

How good is the thinking?

Let's start by focusing on Mattie. How good is her thinking?

◆ Is she giving thinking time?

◆ Is her thinking open?

◆ Is it organized?

◆ Is it deep?

There are certainly indications that she makes time for thinking.

◆ *'I sit and listen and I try to read the signs'…'I didn't say all of that at that meeting. It was going through my mind. I was listening like mad'.*

There are also indications of an openness to possibilities.

◆ *'I thought, what's going on here?'*

◆ *'I guess I decided maybe it was an accident'.*

◆ *'Was I wrong to think that? I don't know'.*

But there are indications of default thinking too, notably when she was tired after a long day. Good thinking is harder when you're weary or under pressure.

◆ 'I thought, "That load of bastards sat at that meeting knowing what they knew about this document during that meeting, the double-crossing conniving…It just reinforced all the paradigms I already had."'

The organization of Mattie's thinking is perhaps the hardest element to see from what she said to us. As we've already pointed out, the way people think tends to be invisible, running for the most part in the background. So what we're saying about her thinking here is inference rather than evidence. Mattie brought a file of e-mails with her and that tells us something about how she organizes her records, but not much about how she organizes her thinking. What organizer or organizers does she use? We don't know. For the moment we can only leave that question open.

But maybe it's the absence of a clear organizer that leaves Mattie, in this case, without the deep understanding that she would have liked. By her own account she didn't have a thorough or coherent sense of what was going on or why.

◆ 'I couldn't believe it. I'm still trying to work out where all the nastiness came from…'

◆ 'I couldn't follow this. I began to lose the thread…'

◆ 'I couldn't understand some of his comments.'

But Mattie's not alone, we suspect. How good is Finn's thinking during all this? Or Kim's? Or Carl's? It is not easy to tell from someone else's account and it would be an inference too far to attempt it. But what we can do is draw out some observations about the nature of thinking when people get together.

Joint thinking

In our angle on good thinking we may have created the impression that thinking is an essentially solitary activity, something you can only do on your own. But of course this isn't the case. Using others as a sounding board, to develop and extend, test and critique our ideas, these are all potentially valuable ways of enlarging and improving our thinking power.

Some of us have a positive preference to develop our thinking in this way. Extroverts (like Graham) for example really like to think socially, in interaction with others. Introverts on the other hand (like Alan) prefer to do more of their thinking internally, inside their own heads. Which is fine. Both approaches can work and we're interested in what works.

But there's a snag. You knew there would be, didn't you?

Actually there are at least a couple. A problem for those of us who are more introverted is that we tend not to make our thinking as open or explicit as extroverts do. The result is that we can leave people having to guess at what we're thinking and often end up being misunderstood as a result. A problem for those of us who are more extroverted is that we tend to do our thinking out loud (or 'through their mouths', as Alan has been known to comment). The result then is that our thinking can be less organized or deep before it goes public.

Now we can learn to deal with these practical problems. At the level of individual thinking and behaviour they are comparatively easy to learn to manage. The difficulty occurs when we're thinking in company.

The problem of social thinking

The problem with thinking in interaction with others – what might be called social thinking – is that it is particularly prone to default. It's simply harder to achieve good thinking in interaction than it is by yourself.

Think about it.

Default thinking is hasty and – we've all experienced it – interactions with others tend to acquire a life of their own. It gets harder to make time for thinking because, while you're doing that, the discussion has swept on relentlessly without you.

Default thinking is narrow and – yes, we've been here too – interactions with others can foster that narrowness, particularly if we are competing for air time and the opportunity to get our point across in the rush of events.

Default thinking is disorganized, and above anything else working with others tends to 'amplify sprawl'. Just think about some of the frustrating meetings you've had to sit through as the discussions meandered on and off the point, checking out most of the available tangents on the way.

Default thinking is shallow and working with others requires more effort to make it deep. It's hard enough sometimes to put a single point across. How much harder to convey a detailed explanation or a chain of logic? You have to get others with you, and keep them with you, as you unfold your reasoning. Herding sheep is difficult enough, but trying to keep a group of independent thinkers together on the same line of thought is hard work.

What's the solution?

There are a couple of answers, at least. One, not surprisingly, is to give time for thinking, to make it an explicit part of your interactions with others. If you need to take 'time out' to ensure the quality of your collective thinking, then say so. The quality of thinking is part of what you have to manage, working by yourself or with others. Now the difficulty with that approach is getting everyone else to come along with you.

Another way is to take a different role in the proceedings. Coach and shape. Detach yourself from immersion in the task and focus on the process. And help others to achieve good thinking. You can do this by asking questions to prompt thinking that is more open, deeper, clearer, more organized.

That's why some people call it 'mental management'. And that's a pretty useful skill to have in a knowledge economy.

Meanwhile, back on Networker…

Good thinking is harder to achieve when other people are involved. And of course other people are involved most of the time in our working lives.

The Networker project is no exception. So let's look at the quality of the thinking, not of Finn and Kim as individuals, but in their interaction, recognizing that we have only a second-hand view of this from Mattie.

Are they making time for thinking together? It doesn't look like it.

They're exchanging e-mails. They seem to be having telephone conversations. But are they making time to jointly think about their thinking, to discuss in an organized way, openly and deeply, how they are thinking about their interaction? It doesn't look like it.

Are they thinking together openly or narrowly?

We can't be sure about their thinking, but what we can observe is that flashpoints seem to occur when their exchanges become narrowly focused rather than open to alternative possibilities.

◆ *'In his view security was the foundation block to the project and had to precede any other criteria.'*

◆ *'Then she goes on to say that this includes using punctuation, paragraphs and sections.'*

Is their thinking together deep, clear and organized?

Again, whatever the quality of their individual thinking, their thinking together seems to demonstrate that two heads are not necessarily better than one. Their dialogue is not using a shared organizer or frame of reference.

◆ *'…asking her to clarify, before he looked at her categories in detail, how she intended to set up the spreadsheet or something.'*

◆ *'…re-send his e-mail with the key points broken out, so she can stand a chance of understanding.'*

The clues are there to be seen. The danger is that they are overlooked in the haste to get things done, or dismissed as a 'clash of personalities' or a 'difficult working relationship' as if these things are an inevitable part of working life rather than issues that we can think and talk our way through.

If we recognize them.

Back to the plot…

We keep interrupting Mattie. In the next episode we're going to get a very different perspective from Kim, but for the moment let's hear what Mattie was thinking by this stage.

And we can listen for clues as to what might happen next.

I went away leaving what I thought was a reasonably tidy situation.

I'd got them to get back in their kennels.

But when I got back from my long weekend my e-mail box was lurid.

This was beginning to upset me. I couldn't get either of them to behave like sensible adults. I'd lost sight of who was right and who was wrong and I just wished they'd both go away.

Because I didn't think these things needed to be worried about until we'd got the clear outline specification.

I suppose what I should have done was to draft a heads of agreement.

We were getting to the point where e-mail and phoning were starting to lose effect, starting to need face-to-face meetings.

I had a meeting about ten days later with Malcolm and Kim and Carl.

We discussed the issues that we felt were in the air, a perfectly amicable meeting. They thought Finn felt they were screwing the Genesis Association. They felt the issue of security had detracted from the development. And they felt disrespect, which was a huge issue for them.

I think these e-mails he sent really upset them.

Malcolm felt we needed clarity over how we move forward and work together in the future.

So what we agreed was that Carl and Kim would send a high-level outline specification which is what the board wanted, a security summary paper, a list of procedural developments and areas for discussion, like access criteria and special payments areas, with a real home-in on funding and pricing and how Malcolm was going to pay his bit.

We were also wondering about using a web server and how much that would cost and Carl was going to provide info on that.

So we were trying to get the thing back on track, but I have to say, though we had this meeting, I just felt some of the pzazz had gone out of it. I don't think I consciously thought 'this is never going to happen', but there didn't seem to be the enthusiasm moving forward that there had been.

I may just have been getting jaded by this time.

to be continued...

complexity

an angle on
complexity
unravelling the plot

Ever wondered what it would be like to be caught up in the middle of a revolution? Suddenly subject to forces you didn't understand. Suddenly not knowing what to expect, not being able to take anything for granted, not even knowing how some of the most basic features of life worked any more. Unexpected interruptions when you were trying to get from A to B, challenged to show your identity.

Welcome to the revolution!

It's been quieter than some, but our lives over the past few decades have been changing dramatically in the technological revolution. Remember when the computer was new and it was thought that the world would only need a handful of them? Remember life before e-mail? Remember life before the call centre? Remember life before the mobile phone? (Yes there was, really.)

These are some of the more obvious features of the revolution. But it has reshaped our lives, and our thinking, in less obvious ways too. Science is dominant. The scientific mindset is dominating. And with a scientific view comes a belief in right and wrong answers, action and reaction, cause and effect. We are encouraged by this to view our lives in a similar way, believing that there is a right way to do things, expecting that our actions will produce predictable responses.

Nowhere is this more true than in the world of organizations and work. How many management books encourage you to follow the 'seven steps (why do there always have to be seven?) to success/happiness/riches/fame etc. etc.'? How many managers devote their time to defining organizational structures, mapping activities, making simplistic links between cause and effect – 'if we cut the price we will sell more', 'if I maintain eye contact, our relationship will improve.' This leads us to think of our businesses, and even ourselves, as machines, with component parts (that need oiling regularly), fixed relationships between the parts and predictable behaviours.

This approach has not only brought great success to the field of science and technology but also to businesses (and business schools!). However it is increasingly limiting our thinking and our actions as our environment grows more complex and less predictable. Think about your own experience for a moment. When you achieved something great, how often did you know exactly what to do and where to go from the start? Or how often have you found that your initial, logical analysis of the situation wasn't enough to get to grips with it? Think of all those times when your plan delivered some of what you wanted, but a load of other stuff as well.

Situations keep changing. We're always trying to get things done in a context that won't stand still.

We are back in the idea-action gap, that unobvious bit between your great concept and its somewhat messier implementation.

In this angle, however, we focus on a particular aspect of this gap, its complexity. In a world increasingly dependent on knowledge and the people who hold it, the ways to get things done are not straightforward.

This complexity is reflected in the nature of this angle. Rather than limit your thinking by simple routines, it presents a number of ideas that will 'come to life' as you apply them. It is only in application to a specific stituation that a defined process can emerge. See the next episode for an example.

Why is this so important for you? Part 1

The end of the last century saw the decline of manufacturing and the growth of the service economy in most western countries. This was accompanied by the rise of the knowledge worker whose contribution has not been through hand skills but 'head skills'. That's why good thinking is such an asset. Today we are in the middle of a war for talent, as human capital becomes the basis of competition for many businesses.

This is great news for you. You have the power. You call the shots.

However, the types of organizations in which we work have also changed. These are businesses that are providing service, interacting with customers. These consumers are increasingly demanding, expecting tailored services to meet their needs. They have the power too. In fact 'they' (the consumer) is 'us' (the worker) on our day(s) off!

Gone are the days for most businesses where known raw material is transformed into standard product and distributed or sold through a single channel. Mass customization is the name of the game and we have to change, to think on the spot, to react, to predict, to deliver. This creates complexity and we need to handle it as providers.

It's not like we all want the same thing any more. Henry Ford's colour card, 'any colour you want so long as it's black', seems incredible, a relic from consumer pre-history. Now we have choice. Consumer markets produce a baffling array of products to fuel this. This creates complexity and we need to handle it as consumers.

We are given less direction by society in making these choices. The institutions of norms and values – the government, the church, marriage, local communities, professions – are all less influential. You have the choice. This creates complexity and we need to handle it as individuals.

Choice and power, a heady combination. But a world of complexity. So being personally effective is still a challenge. Actually it's more of a challenge than ever.

Being personally effective is making viable choices, using your power to make things happen. But the old, quick answers are gone. There are no reliable short-hand approaches. Habits don't work. The context keeps changing, last time's successful strategy doesn't work this time.

So what do you do?

Simply, get in amongst it.

Don't ignore the complexity. Expect it. Go looking for it. Work with it. Do what you can to understand your situation from many different viewpoints. Think about how your situations have developed over time. Think about how they might continue to unfold from here. Be open to possibilities. Explore them. Look for the obvious and the unobvious. Map the issues. Think about links and interdependencies, about how the whole system works. Generate options. Anticipate their consequences. In short, create a rich understanding. And, vitally, with this understanding do something. Then watch. Listen. Think again. React.

Perhaps that sounds like a lot to remember. But what does the previous paragraph amount to? It isn't designed to be a sequence of 20 steps that you have to remember and follow to manage complexity. It's easy enough to get overwhelmed by complexity without having to overload our attention with all that extra mental baggage. We need to bring simplification to complexity. So what's the shape below the detail in that last paragraph? Basically two ideas: making sense and making use. Something we introduced in our first angle. Two things to bear in mind, not seven, not 20. Active thinking and thoughtful action.

Let's illustrate how you can use these to get to grips with complexity. And let's start with an organizer. In the spirit of simplification, we'll make it an icon. A simple picture that's easy to keep in mind. And in the spirit of working with complexity, we won't explain the icon…yet. See what you think.

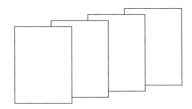

Getting in the 'right' frame of mind

Have you driven a car in a foreign country? Odd isn't it. All those things you take for granted changed slightly. Road signs are in different places. Perhaps you have to drive on the other side of the road. Maybe the steering wheel is on the wrong side so that you're changing gear with the other hand. Other drivers behave in unfamiliar ways. Protocols are not the same. You can still drive, but it takes concentration, it's hard work. Just when you think you've got it sussed, you make a silly mistake.

Driving is a complex thing, made easy because we do most of it automatically or unconsciously once we've learned how. But in a slightly changed situation the old routines don't quite work, so much more conscious attention is required. It is hard not to slip back into those old habits. You have to get into the right 'frame of mind'.

A consequence of complexity is that every situation can be viewed and described in multiple ways.

No single perspective is complete. Organizations are human networks, we all interpret what we see, filtering information through our experience. There are no single right answers to problems and challenges in this territory.

What's more, the environment is constantly on the move, so just as approaches become 'automatic', habits, the situation changes. And then, just like driving abroad, we make a silly mistake.

If there is no single right answer, does that mean that there are no wrong ones either? Thinking in terms of right and wrong is perhaps not a helpful starting point. In this sort of complex space, the space where we live and work these days, there are many possible routes and choices at every point on the journey towards your goal. Furthermore as you progress you will learn more and may come to realize you were heading for the wrong goal in the first place!

Of course, taking action requires you to narrow down these choices. One option is to go with the first apparently sensible route or decision. This may be based on your experiences of 'similar' situations or the advice of an experienced colleague, or it might be the only thing you can see, a product of default thinking: hasty, narrow, superficial, disorganized. In fact, you may not even be aware of the decision you are making, it could be automatic, unconscious, like driving a car.

We argue that, working in complex situations, you constantly need to be generating options, to give yourself choice. The starting point for this is to ask, what can you see in the world around you and, critically, how could you creatively challenge that view?

Picture it

One technique for generating new perspectives and choices is the use of metaphors. You probably first came across the metaphor studying language – 'the nurse was an angel' – a way of asserting that something is (or is like) something else. This approach is much more significant than a mere descriptive device, a convenient linguistic shorthand. It also determines the way we see or think about a situation.

Gareth Morgan, in his book *Images of Organization* (Sage Publications, 1997), applies this idea of metaphor to the analysis of organizations. He makes the point that thinking about the workplace is restricted by the metaphor of 'organizations as machines'. He goes on to describe seven other ways of thinking about, or metaphors for, organizations, including organizations as organisms, brains, cultures, instruments of domination and political systems. (We take a political perspective in our next angle.) Each metaphor brings different insights to the process of understanding complex situations and how they work.

This chapter (and book for that matter) subscribes to this 'multi-perspective' approach. The more views the better. They enable us to build a rich picture, and a deeper understanding, of the situation.

How do you use metaphors?

One way is directly, to check or challenge the assumptions that lie behind your immediate sense of the situation you are facing. Ask:

◆ 'What metaphor is implied by my current view?'

◆ 'How am I limiting my thinking?'

Metaphors can be so embedded in our own view of the world that using someone else to ask these types of questions may help. Tell them your perspective. Ask them to tell you what it sounds like to them. They may uncover your metaphor more readily than you can. It's a great way of harvesting clues.

Another option to liberate and open your thinking is to apply an unusual metaphor to your situation.

This has become popular in the area of creative thinking. Questions like:

◆ 'If my problem were an animal, what kind of animal would it be?'

◆ 'If my situation were to be described on national television news…?'

◆ 'If Mickey Mouse explained what was going on…?'

Having done this, step back. What does this tell me? Why did I think of this issue as a shark? Mickey focused on the people aspects, have I been ignoring these?

All seems a bit silly, doesn't it?

There are good reasons why it can help.

Our brain is an incredible thinking tool. Much of its power lies out of our direct awareness. It is not conscious. It is unconscious. Your unconscious mind is at work when you are driving a car. This is why all the decisions you take seem automatic. They are still being made, but not in a way that you notice.

How do you access something you are not aware of?

This can be particularly tricky as our conscious thinking, that rational cause and effect process, can get in the way. So you can't think your way there. This is where metaphors come in. They allow you to bypass the logic and get to the unconscious mind. That's why it feels silly. It's not logical, deliberately.

The unconscious mind deals effectively in 'wholes'. Whereas your conscious thinking is excellent for deconstructing a situation, seeing its components, unconsciously you can deal with the whole picture, get a sense of how it hangs together. Describing the situation as an animal is one way of getting at this holistic picture, because the choice of animal won't simply be by chance. It's a way of accessing the pattern behind the details, and getting some sense of its overall implications. It's a mental move that gives you another 'take' on complexity. You can then consciously analyze that take, ask why this particular animal, what features are relevant, how do they interrelate, what do they signify?

So when you're dealing with complexity, and the detail becomes too much to hold in your head, you can't get your mind round it to make sense of it, come at it from another direction. Try a different metaphor. Picture your situation differently.

Also this can be fun, which is always good.

Talking of fun, techniques which ask you to draw pictures, write poems, build clay models all have the same process at their heart. But perhaps your work is messy enough without going as far as the clay.

The closest you get to your unconscious is when you're asleep. Dreams are an unconscious device. Getting insight into a problem by waking at 3a.m. is not uncommon. Your unconscious at work again.

Can you remember the last time you dreamed about a work-related problem or opportunity? How did you picture it in your dream? Or, if we asked you to do a drawing of an issue that you're facing now, what would you draw? How would you picture it?

But what is the right picture?

None of them and all of them. They should all give some insight, perhaps some more than others, some at different times than others.

So which should I use?

We have a pragmatic view on this. Use the one(s) that are most useful. That may sound trite, but in itself it reflects our metaphor for working with complexity, that is a journey with many viable routes to the answer, one where every time you take a step the world can suddenly appear a very different place. So keep moving.

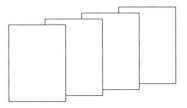

Generate choices

Reframing is a technique closely related to the use of metaphor. It has been particularly developed in the school of neuro-linguistic programming (NLP).

The approach asks you to put an event or situation in a different context. Change one or more components or features. See how the situation looks now. Change the time, the place, the characters, the basic assumptions. This can be great fun. Much humour is reframing, putting the common in an uncommon setting. (Think of Gary Larson's Far Side cartoons – dogs driving cars, sheep having parties, talking cows.)

In a world where many of the features of a situation are assumptions or facts open to interpretation (like most!) this is a valuable way of exploring different options. Ask yourself:

◆ 'If this assumption wasn't true and its opposite was, then what would the situation look like?'

◆ 'What if we only had half the time for this or twice the money (yeah right!)?'

◆ 'If Indiana Jones was leading this project, what would he do?'

…and so on.

One area in which we naturally make assumptions is about the attitudes and intentions of other people (and them of us).

Often we see someone's behaviour in light of how we believe they feel about our project or us. Try reframing your assumptions about people's attitudes:

◆ 'If she was my biggest fan, how would I interpret her behaviour now?'

◆ 'Let me assume he's genuinely trying to help. What would that tell me about the way I'm going about this?'

Try it. Think about an idea that you're trying to put into action. Think about someone whose 'attitude' seems to be getting in the way. Ask yourself these sorts of questions. Come up with at least two other ways in which you might move forward from where you are now.

In summary, metaphors and reframing are ways of generating new ideas and options.

Metaphors work in a holistic way, encouraging your unconscious mind to integrate the issues you face, then giving you the opportunity to deconstruct the metaphoric picture and learn more. Reframing allows you to change assumptions and test the impact. Play around with key variables, such as:

◆ time (or timing);

◆ location;

◆ characters involved;

◆ money (or other resources);

◆ outcomes (or products).

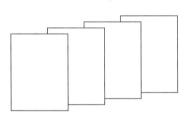

Anticipate consequences

What's that you say? *'Oh no! I thought it was complex before, but now I have ten new ways of looking at my problem and a dozen options. Now it really is complex.'*

Good. Operating in a complex world means living with, and working with, the complexity, not just seeking to simplify it. Not yet anyway. Uncertainty doesn't always feel comfortable. Especially when the boss, or the client, is pushing for an answer. Holding back from seeking a solution too soon is an important capability – an idea we will be returning to in the next episode.

Metaphors and reframing allow you to view your situation from different perspectives. To generate data. They are examples of divergent thinking. You start with a viewpoint and generate more and more options. You now need to find a basis on which they converge, to a decision, an action.

You've generated some options. Actually that's not so hard to do, at least once we turn our attention to it. Leaping to solutions is something that comes easily to us. You will have seen people doing that. So, brainstorm some options? Sure. We can do that.

Okay, now here's the tricky bit. Choosing among those options.

Not so hard, if the world were standing still. Then we would simply establish our decision criteria, assess our options against those criteria. Make an informed and rational decision. And proceed. Pass GO. Collect £200.

If only our world were standing still. But it isn't and that's the other dimension of complexity that we need to keep in mind. Complexity is not just a matter of volume, it's also a matter of movement. There are a lot of factors at work and they interact and go on interacting so that the patterns shift, conditions escalate, fade or even disappear.

Peter Senge at the Massachusetts Institute of Technology wrote one of the business bestsellers of the 1990s, *The Fifth Discipline* (Doubleday, 1990), on this subject. Underpinning much of his approach was the concept of 'systems thinking'. Basically this is an approach to looking at situations from a holistic perspective, taking into account all (or many) of the factors influencing the situation, critically considering the interactions between these factors and the 'systems' that are formed as a consequence.

At the heart of systems thinking is the concept of feedback.

That is, an element in a system impacts another element that in turn affects the first element. Or another way, the consequences of our action often impact on the original action.

There are two basic types of feedback, that which increases (or reinforces) the original action and that which decreases (or limits) it.

Senge drew attention to the impact of the time delay that often exists between taking an action and seeing the consequences (intended and otherwise) of that action. Too often we expect instant impact from our interventions and may overcompensate or give up when we don't get an immediate response.

The Fifth Discipline contains detailed descriptions of typical systemic patterns. These archetypes, as Senge calls them, form the building blocks for creating systems maps. This is definitely a powerful approach, but we believe you can make significant progress in managing complexity just by considering feedback (reinforcing and limiting) and delays.

How?

Here are some simple examples.

Did you have a shower this morning? Sorry to be so personal. When you turned on the taps, did the water come through at exactly the temperature you wanted? Or did you have to adjust them? And when you adjusted them (gave the system some feedback), how long was it before the water was coming through at the right temperature?

Trying to steer a trolley in a DIY store or a supermarket illustrates the same principle. Between the intention (turn to avoid this obstacle) and the outcome (wheeled monster actually turning) there is often a gap. Which we fill with exasperation, embarrassment, apology and so on. The idea-action gap strikes again. Until we learn to expect it and factor the delay into the timing of our steering. Complex systems thinking at work!

Want an everyday human example? You are trying to persuade someone to accept an idea. You make your case and they listen, perhaps keenly. Maybe they even tell you that they personally like what you're saying and that they will get back to you. Fair enough. But then they don't get back to you as quickly as you expect or would wish (well, quick answers are usually no). So you call again, make your case a bit more forcefully, turn up the transmit dial. And this time they seem less enthusiastic, so you push a bit more…and eventually they say no. Were they just messing you around from the start? Probably not. Maybe you just didn't factor in the time they needed to think through all the implications of what you'd been saying, or to persuade the other people that they would have to involve in order to go ahead.

So next time you're in the shower and the water is too hot or too cold, use that as a cue to think about some intractable work-related issue from a systems perspective.

These are small examples, but they give you the building blocks for systems thinking. Being alert to the possibility of these patterns can significantly raise your ability to make sense of complex situations.

In an important sense it gets our thinking moving.

This is because the type of complexity we need to master is not 'detail complexity', that is difficulty arising from the scale of a problem that has to be solved and therefore the volume of issues. It is 'dynamic complexity', where it is the interrelationships of issues and their behaviour and impact over time that need to be considered. This gets us thinking ahead, not just thinking about our choices but also anticipating their consequences.

Imagine a tree in winter, not an evergreen but one where you can see the tangle of trunk, branches and twigs. That's detail complexity. Now think about the tree as a system. As the seasons change, the leaves come into bud and then open, flowers appear and maybe fruit of some sort. Then the leaves fall off again. That's dynamic complexity. Actually, that's the visible part of dynamic complexity. Don't forget the less visible stuff that's going on as well, sap rising and falling, roots drawing in water and nutrients, photosynthesis (now we're into the subtle stuff) in the leaves.

So the point of this metaphor is…?

Once you've generated a range of choices, different branches that you might follow through the complexity, remember that your tree is changing too. Think about that before you commit yourself. When you're trying to understand how something works, look for multiple causes, not just one. And when you're trying to think through how a situation will develop, look for multiple consequences, not just one.

complexity

clued up

momentum

Look ahead for the consequences of the consequences, the repercussions.

Make a mental model of how your complex situation works. Or how it might work. You won't necessarily be sure. That's part of the complexity. And any model is a simplification. That's okay. You're between a rock and a hard place here. The rock is making it too simplistic so that it doesn't reflect reality. The hard place is making it so elaborate that you can't understand it. You're looking for a level that makes your complexity manageable.

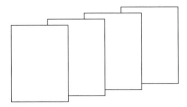

Keep moving

There is a risk here. Analysis paralysis. The approaches we have described are deliberately 'loose' – there are many ways in which they can be used. You need to pitch them right for your situation. The aim is to enrich your thinking about the space that you have to navigate. The idea-action gap. But don't think for too long. Or put even better, don't think while stationary. Use the rich picture to narrow down your options and choose a sensible next action, perhaps one that is common to a couple of favourite routes. Then JDI. Just do it.

There is no right step. First, because the total is too complicated to fully understand. Second, it is all open to personal interpretation. Third, if that wasn't enough, it keeps changing. So standing still doesn't help. The world will move around you. You risk becoming stuck. Let go of the view that you should have it all planned first.

Keep moving. It will open up new perspectives.

It will give you new vantage points. (Ever thought about the relationship between the words advance and advantage?)

Keep moving. It will suggest more choices and bring you closer to seeing their consequences.

Keep moving. That is the key action (more on action in the next two angles).

Now you are on the move, two critical things.

Take small steps. For all the reasons above.

Keep your eyes, ears, in fact every sensory receptor open. You need feedback. What happens when you act will be vital data in continuing to build your model of the world in which you are operating. Pick up all the clues. If you don't you have wasted your move. A giant game of *Cluedo*.

So standing back from all this…

Why is this so important for you? Part 2

In all the angles we have been suggesting ways to make you more conscious of your thinking and, critically, what is going on around you. This is to heighten your awareness, make you more conscious of the clues available.

In this chapter we have also been saying, trust your gut feel, your unconscious. At first sight this may appear contradictory. However this rather reflects a sequence of understanding, of learning. Think back to our driving example. How much conscious attention was required when you first got into a car? You probably had to concentrate very hard just to co-ordinate depressing the clutch, moving the gear stick and not veering wildly into the middle of the road as you clung tightly to the steering wheel. And now we suspect you could drive past your motorway junction on the way to work

complexity

clued up

momentum

because your conscious attention was totally focused on the coming activities of the day.

Our learning moves from conscious to unconscious. It is our limited conscious that prevents us from spotting the clues, but there is plenty of unconscious power available. It is as you work with these ideas in the context of your own real situations, and as they begin to form part of your (informed) unconscious repertoire, that you will build your real effectiveness. But beware of old habits. You have to keep re-informing your unconscious, building a richer repertoire.

We have continued to stress this need to open up our thinking, not to get caught in our usual habits and patterns. This will feel awkward to start with, unnatural. It also requires you to live with more ambiguity and uncertainty. To allow issues to remain unresolved, until the time is right. Oh, and also to take action more quickly and frequently.

Hmm.

A bit of a dichotomy here, leave things undecided and act. Yep, that's right.

How the hell does all that work then?

The key is to know what is certain and to know it really, really well. The main (if not the only) absolute is you and where you're coming from, what you believe in most.

Whoa, it's gone all New Age again!

Definitely not. Just back to our original premise. You have choice and power. How do you make a choice if you don't know what you want? Particularly when you can't fit the problem on to your spreadsheet and write a macro to solve it. What you want is rooted in what you value and in what you believe.

This is good news and bad news.

The good is that with no right answers (and therefore no wrong ones!) it is legitimate to go for what you want, for you. The bad news is you need to be clear about what you want (what you really, really want). Most of us aren't.

And there's another source of complexity that you have to handle, characteristic of human systems, and that we will turn to in our angle on politics.

What about that icon?

What did you make of our complexity icon then?

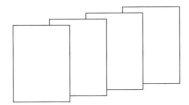

Perhaps nothing. Perhaps you made your own instead. That would be good.

Here's what ours says to us.

It's a storyboard. Complex situations are stories that unfold over time. One thing leads to another. It's a moving picture. We need to look for that.

It's a series of frames. Complex situations can be, and need to be, examined from a variety of perspectives.

It's a set of elements. Some are more prominent than others. Some are in the foreground, while others are in the background. The parts are separate and yet related at the same time.

It's partly visible, partly hidden. We need to look beyond what is readily apparent and take into account the bits that are less obvious.

complexity

clued up

momentum

And it's a way of reminding us to pay attention to four activities when we're dealing with complexity:

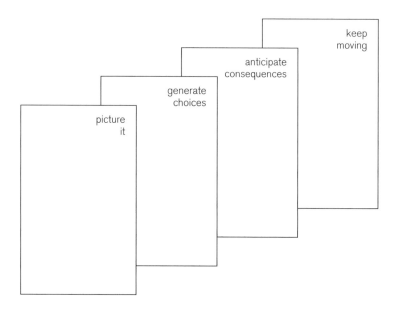

an episode on
complexity

In our introduction we said that throughout the book there would be a shift in nature. As we got further through the book, more of the emphasis would be on you working on your 'stuff', rather than us providing a context for you to see the ideas we present in action. Well, you are now entering the second half, so you might reasonably expect a change of some sort.

We are going to ease you in gently in this episode. We will still be using the context of Networker, but we will be asking you to be much more active with the material presented. Was that a groan we heard? Not one of those chapters where they give you lots of exercises and want you to think as well as read!

Yep!

The complexity material presented in the preceding angle really comes to life when you apply it. Some of it might have seemed obvious, trite even. The frameworks and ideas used are deliberately straightforward. The complexity already exists in the world to which you will apply these ideas. The aim of the ideas presented is to simplify so that you can see the patterns in the complexity. This way you can choose actions, recognizing consequences which allow for the rich nature of the environment but help you to make sense of it. For each situation, your approach will emerge from the elements described in the complexity angle.

To see this at work you have to apply these ideas to a complex situation. Before letting them loose on your own world (unless of course you have been particularly keen and have already applied all the ideas suggested), we would like you to help Kim and Carl on their Networker project.

If you have read the previous two episodes you will know that things have not been going as smoothly as they might.

In fact, by the point where the previous episode left off, Kim has recognized the need for some help. Yours.

In this episode we ask you to advise Kim and Carl on the best way forward with the project and encourage you to use some of the ideas presented in the complexity angle (and the earlier ones as well). We will be giving some examples ourselves of the tools in action, but we do encourage you to have a go first.

Your consultancy brief

A friend of a friend has recommended that Kim talks to you. Your friend (who needs enemies when…) knows you as someone with an interest in getting things done in the messy modern world and believes you can put your momentum behind Kim and Carl.

You have agreed to help Kim. While you don't know her, you do see the problems she is facing as a good vehicle for your own learning and people like Kim and Carl are always useful to know.

Kim has left a voice-mail, which concludes with the two basic questions on which she is looking for help:

- 'Where are we going wrong?'
- 'What should our next steps be?'

In response you have asked Kim if she can give you some of the background on what has happened so far. She explains that she and Carl remain committed to the project but are coming to believe that Finn is trying to scupper it. They are finding the working environment increasingly untenable and recently instigated an open and frank meeting with Mattie and Malcolm to air the issues and get their help. Kim has promised you an e-mail attachment laying out the key events from her point of view. She also suggests a conversation with Carl and, if you can, Mattie. (In other words, if you haven't read the previous two episodes, now might be a good time!) Kim doesn't want you to have only her viewpoint.

Kim also offers a telephone conversation but asks, as time is short, that you read the background e-mail attachment first. The transcript of that conversation follows.

However, before turning to the details of Kim's e-mail attachment and the transcript, just pause to consider how you might have handled the call with Kim. The later chapters will focus more on this area, but imagine you were about to make the call to Kim.

Think about:

◆ In what sort of frame of mind do you expect to find Kim?

◆ How are you going to build trust and rapport quickly?

◆ What is your opening line going to be? Write it down.

◆ How will you know when to stop?

These can be key moments. We never get a second chance to make a first impression. Apply good thinking.

Players:	1	Kim and Carl	Webcom Ltd
	2	Malcolm McNeill	Director of Genesis Centre
	3	Mattie	Vice chair, Genesis Association – alumni body
	4	Association board	Governing body of the Genesis Association
	5	Project sub-group	Mattie, Finn, Saheena, Malcolm, Carl, Kim
	6	Finn	Member of sub-group
	7	Saheena	Member of sub-group
	8	Jenny	Manager, Genesis Centre
	9	Alumni	Alumni to whom Networker concept presented
	10	Alumni conference	Conference for all alumni

Date	From	To	Event	Key points
January	1	2	Conversation in bar	Had recently returned to UK and were considering seeking work – frustrated at difficulty of identifying appropriate colleagues who could help. Very informally discussed possibility of creating effective networking tools ourselves. (This led to our spending next 4 mths creating two websites for Genesis Centre.)
Feb–April	1		Development	Further explored concept and potential of interactive community environment for the Centre, developing general framework and coming up with the name Networker. Also started pursuing marketing and media opportunities for using Networker to promote the programme, Genesis Centre and the Association.
23 April ongoing	1	9	E-mail and Excel sheet	Well before presenting Networker concept officially, started collating topics for Networker searches such as areas of special interest or particular expertise and gathering suggestions for other search criteria, inc geography, industry, etc.
May	2	3	Phone/ face to face	Malcolm appraised Mattie of our informal, very high-level conversations and invited her to a meeting at which we would present the concept and its potential as a viable project. There was, apparently, concern that this might be a threat to the Association.
21 May	1	2 3	Document	Introduced concept of Networker, describing its value and exploring potential content; it was stressed that this was opportunity for the Centre and Association to work together to support alumni.
22 May	1	2 3 8	Meeting	It was explained that this was first time this concept was formally presented to either the Centre or Association. 17/4 papers discussed; underlying principles agreed; concept, respect and protection of IPR discussed, understood and (verbally) accepted. Surprise was expressed that we were being so 'paranoid'.

complexity

clued up

momentum

Date	From	To	Event	Key points
1 June	1	3	E-mail	Request for copy of Association database to allow preparation for 4/6 mtg.
1 June	3	1	E-mail	Refusal, copied to board, implying that there was something inappropriate in our request.
4–5 June	3	1	Meeting at Association office	Explanation by Mattie of Centre/Association history and some reasons for the fear/animosity, stressing personal willingness to move forward but admitting reservations. Explanation of 1/6 negative e-mail. More detailed explanation by us of Networker concept, background, potential, value, etc.
7 June	1	4	Association board mtg	We described Networker concept, need, potential, value, etc. Meeting was constructive until mention of development in partnership with the Centre; very acrimonious and heated discussion followed – after which we felt the two bodies could not work together (despite their apparent recognition of the value the Networker community would have to both organizations, and to alumni).
8 June	1	10	Association conference	We made presentations to the alumni during all breaks, receiving a very enthusiastic and positive response. A survey indicated that nearly 90% would use Networker. (We have since received many encouraging e-mails.)
8 June	4	2	Association board mtg with Malcolm	Association board met with Malcolm to try to rebuild relationship.
9 June	4	1	Association board mtg	We met with board and were made aware of previous evening's mtg with Malcolm, which encouraged us to believe there was a commitment to partnership. Sub-group established to enable rapid development of Networker. The possibility of staged payments was discussed in recognition of our willingness to undertake this work for little above costs.
20 June	1	5	Various docs	Paper describing Networker concept, experience, differentiators, security, opportunities, etc. Did not expressly state the ownership on IPR as it was (we thought) clear that this point had been previously agreed by Association board at 7/6 and 9/6 mtgs. (Genesis Centre has never been at issue.)
21 June	6	1	E-mail	Finn raised some good points on security but did not link back to the original paper, which had addressed the majority of them already. Despite board's decision to create the sub-group to facilitate rapid

Date	From	To	Event	Key points
				development, his suggestions were, apparently, intended to delay the process.
21 June	1	5	Various docs	We created and distributed a detailed (5-page) paper identifying and evaluating threats to security and the likely risk of occurrence. Alternative options were presented and a recommendation made – with clear rationale.
21 June	5	1	E-mail	Immediate response from Finn, not responding to the points made but raising unrelated ones.
21 June	5	1	Phone conversation	Lengthy but unproductive phone conversation in which we tried to understand the underlying causes of Finn's discomfort. He seemed unable to articulate them and unwilling to listen to the points we were making.
23 June	1	3	E-mail	I copied Finn's unclear response to Mattie requesting her assistance in resolving.
23 June	5	4	E-mail & documents	Finn distributed a paper to all board members, again raising issues that were being handled by the sub-group – predominantly security-related – implying that we were avoiding them.
24 June	1	3	E-mail	We restated our commitment to the project but explained that the current working environment was untenable. Development work was put on hold until we could speak with Mattie (who was on holiday for a week).
9 July	1	2 3	Mtg	Open and frank mtg between Mattie, Malcolm and ourselves.

(Did you read that spreadsheet or did you skip over it? That's often the temptation with complexity. So that spreadsheet is an illustration as well as a source of data.)

You open the conversation with Kim, asking about how the meeting with Malcolm and Mattie had gone and what had happened since.

The meeting Carl and I had with Malcolm and Mattie was really for us to tell Mattie, 'Under the current conditions we do not feel that we can move forward.' Mattie, again, very good, constructive, 'Well we'll wait until the board meeting, we'll invite Finn to remove himself from the board as his behaviour has been unacceptable. Don't worry Kim and Carl, we want this to happen, all the board is behind you.'

Now at this point, which we didn't know at the time but Mattie did, Finn had constructed a questionnaire. And you know how you can define what answer you are going to get by the question you ask. So Finn had constructed this questionnaire along the lines of 'Do you think there should be some security of individual's data or that everything should be totally insecure?' And, of course, there is only one way to answer a question like that and it gives people the impression that we are totally unconcerned about security. And there were ten questions all worded in a similar way, about web hosting or whatever. But we didn't know this at the time.

So about three days before the board meeting we had prepared the demo we were going to take with us and Saheena had gone on holiday. Actually I was very pissed off with Saheena because she had chosen that week, having just become a board member, she had chosen that week to go away. Saheena doesn't like conflict at the best of times. So I suspect — and I have no basis for my suspicion but I suspect — the fact that she wasn't going to have to be at the board meeting — because it was going to be a difficult meeting — could have had an influence on Saheena's decision not to be there.

Malcolm had decided not to be at the meeting. Malcolm was unable to be at the meeting because it was the last day of a programme. So there was going to be this board meeting with all these people who had seen Finn's questionnaire and I didn't even know about the questionnaire at this point.

Two or three days before the board meeting I got an e-mail from Finn, saying 'Oh by the way, Kim, I just thought you would like to see the questionnaire that I put out to all the other board members.' He hadn't published the results, but he had got everyone else's results, but he wrote in such a way, you know, 'I discussed this with Mattie and we agreed we should distribute it.' So I forwarded his note to Mattie, saying, 'He is either representing you inappropriately or…if he is not then I would like to understand.' She came back saying that 'we had discussed it, but no way had I agreed he could send it out', which was kind of confusing as she had filled it in.

It made me reassess again.

First I got a copy of the questionnaire, then I got Mattie saying she hadn't been aware that he had distributed it, then I got his collated responses that included hers.

I read through those responses and only one person had given a rational response, saying 'You can't answer a question phrased like that' – everyone else had dignified it with a response.

I think this might be the final straw. It isn't so much Finn's behaviour, Mattie trying to be on both sides. It is that, if this is the feeling of the board, they cannot recognize that this is a deliberate attempt to scupper the project, then I cannot continue working with them.

complexity

Picture it

Well, a complex picture. So what do you do now?

The temptation may be to leap to some answers. Perhaps you already have. Remember we are 'hardwired' to make sense of the information presented to us and that often means drawing quick conclusions. Best to think of these as early hypotheses!

Step one is to hold back from these conclusions. This is a situation, in the gap, that requires good thinking. So firstly, 'give it time' and be 'open' in your thinking.

Remember the next two?

Organized and deep.

clued up

momentum

So let's get organized.

This means managing all the data you have, and you've got lots. Some of it is factual, some opinion, and we suspect some completely imagined. Be careful – the way you choose to organize the data can often presuppose an answer. Have you ever bought something on impulse and then come up with the rationale for the decision? You always manage to come to the conclusion it was a good idea! So be open at this stage, beware of simply working back from the answer.

Use the next page, it's blank. The page after contains where we have had a go at making sense of this complexity, but you may learn more if you do it from scratch for yourself. What is more, you'll probably see something we haven't – no right answers here!

What did we think?

Well, we are about to contradict (slightly) our previous advice, that of not jumping to conclusions. What these quick conclusions often represent is your unconscious processing of the data. You don't 'see' the analysis (it is unconscious!), but you do see an answer. This can be very useful. After all, our 'brain power' is largely unconscious and it is one of the (only) ways to deal with the large amount of data presented in this messy world. Our earlier advice was a recommendation to organize the data first, in a sense, to help your unconscious see the patterns and draw accurate conclusions. Patterns – we use the plural deliberately because there are bound to be many possible answers and we encourage you to consider several choices, not just one.

So what does this mean practically?

We have a suggested 'halfway house'. Remember in the angle on complexity we talked about the use of metaphors? Well, they are one way of drawing conclusions without limiting your thinking about other possibilities.

There is something about the slightly absurd nature of a metaphor that allows us to hold a picture without over-committing to it.

Try it. As you think of the Networker story, what image or picture comes to mind? Go with your immediate thoughts, bypass the conscious, go straight to the unconscious.

◆ Is there any sound with the picture?

◆ What about feelings? Or other senses?

Now reflect on the picture…

◆ What are the key features?

◆ How do they relate to the story?

◆ What was your mind playing at when it presented you with this picture?

This is getting the rational part of your brain working on the new information presented.

A swarm of bees.

That is what popped into our heads (well, one of our heads, you get close when writing a book together, but not that close).

So what was this picture saying to us?

- ◆ Lots of people.
- ◆ Lots of noise.
- ◆ Movement, but 'chaotic' rather than clearly purposeful.
- ◆ Anger.
- ◆ High potential for productivity, impact, progress, powerfulness.

And so on.

This approach can be useful before the more systematic analysis of the data as a way of picking up important themes or issues around which to centre your thinking.

Relationships – that's a theme that jumps out to us. There seem to be a lot of them and they keep changing. Perhaps there are some patterns.

Mapping is a good way to spot patterns. Choosing an effective way of mapping is again more about intuition than technique. Often it is good to simply start playing. It's a way of exploring, of thinking adventurously. You may find this daunting to start with, so we've provided a process that has worked for us, if you need it.

1 Use big paper, A3 at least, landscape. Have a pack of coloured pens.

2 Pick an area – an easy one first, say, 'key influencers'.

3 What are the principal dimensions I want to represent with my map? How will I represent those? For 'key influencers' that might be time on the project (represented by size of text), quality of relationship with other influencers (distance apart), attitude to project (colour of text) and so on.

4 Put a key element in the middle of the page. In our example, perhaps one of the players.

5 Get drawing. Let your imagination go. Feel free to add things that pop into your head. Your unconscious mind will love this.

6 Pause. Have you missed anything? Were your starting dimensions complete? Add more.

7 Stand back. What is this saying? What are the major risks? What can this person do to influence things?

8 Pick another theme. Repeat.

9 How do these two maps interrelate? What did you forget on the first map?

10 And so on.

Well, we promised some 'data organizing' of our own. We picked up the
theme of relationships and came up with the following.

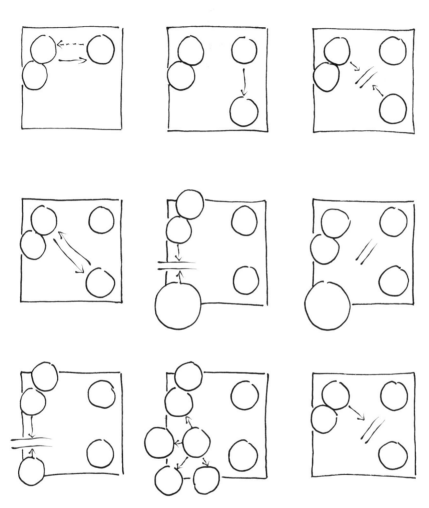

You may be thinking that we have moved into Oriental rug design (or perhaps that we should!). This is what developed as we started to map the interactions. How did we come up with this? The honest answer is it just happened, but the post-rationalized view (or the conscious interpretation of our unconscious approach) is that:

◆ we had the notion of a playing field (the square) and the players involved (the bubbles);

◆ we wanted to show movements and how relationships developed over time, hence the series of squares (our 'storyboard');

◆ we wanted to get an overall picture of the pattern of interactions, therefore chose arrows and lines.

We have reproduced this to show how it actually happened and have not labelled it to make it easier for you to read. The important thing is to see the principle of how mapping can be helpful rather than get into the specifics of this example. However, we can imagine not having some sort of key for the diagram might be causing you some frustration, so:

◆ Kim and Carl are the bubbles in the top left of each square;

◆ Malcolm is top right;

◆ Mattie is bottom right;

◆ the Association committee is the large bubble on the bottom left;

◆ Finn appears as the individual bubble on the bottom left;

◆ the arrows represent the interaction, dashed arrows being weaker or reluctant engagement;

◆ the two parallel lines represent a breakdown in effective communication.

So what did it say to us?

First, a word of caution.

We are basing this analysis on the accounts we have. And you've already seen how they differ. So you need to be careful about drawing conclusions, especially about individuals whose accounts of the situation you haven't heard.

- Lots of breakdowns in communication – five out of the nine windows.

- The players 'stay in their corners'. Looking back at the table of data there is a hidden clue. There is a lot of e-mail communication. The key players rarely meet and when they do it tends to be in big 'set piece' meetings. One of the few 'intimate' meetings (4/5 June) goes very well (second box down on the left on the Oriental rug).

- Kim takes the initiative on many occasions (arrows come from her). Changes in energy or movement on the project are initiated by Kim.

Another hunch is emerging as we work through the analysis. Kim and Carl have a big stake in this project. They have chosen to put their livelihoods on the line for this project, or at least the business they are looking to build around it. It is, therefore, not surprising that they are driving the pace. However, how would you assess their clients' commitment to this? How important is it to Mattie or Malcolm? While it's an important project for both of them, neither Mattie nor Malcolm has the same sort of stake in this as Kim and Carl.

Our hunch is that the fluctuations in direction and energy of the project bear a fairly direct relationship to the motivation of Kim and Carl. We don't have quite enough data to test this assumption, but a careful conversation with Kim or Carl about how they were feeling at the key turning points in the story would quickly provide some evidence.

Again this could be mapped, simply plotting motivation against time and marking the key events of the project.

Let us assume that this did show a relationship. This will allow us to look at an approach to generating a view of how the future may look.

Generate choices

We have generated from our mapping two key dimensions for the success of this venture. These are not necessarily the only two. Your analysis may have identified others. However, we do feel that these are significant themes, namely:

- quality of relationships between those involved;

- level of motivation of Kim and Carl.

Assuming these factors underpin any future that may emerge, we can explore the possibilities by characterizing the extreme combinations. A sketch can quickly yield insights.

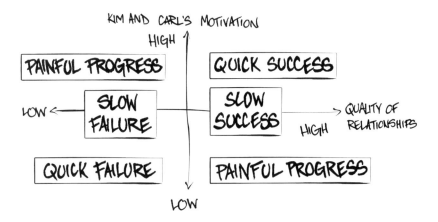

We have plotted on the axes possible scenarios that might be the result of the different conditions. These scenarios presume that:

◆ the success or failure of the project depends heavily on the quality of relationships;

◆ the speed at which the project develops is significantly influenced by Kim and Carl's motivation;

◆ an extreme of either dimension will be sufficient to keep the project alive in the absence of the other, but progress will be painful.

As an aside, don't forget this trick of creating a 2x2 matrix (or 3x3, if you want to draw some finer distinctions. Just remember to keep it manageable). It's a great way of shifting your thinking up from isolated factors to patterns of interaction, and so of working with more complexity. Use your chosen dimensions as axes, to create four quadrants, each representing a combination of the extremes of your dimensions. Think about what happens in each area. What choices do they represent? And what are the implications of these choices? What are the consequences?

So what did your mapping of the data reveal?

Did underpinning dimensions emerge? If so, do they provide a useful framework to look at potential outcomes?

Choices and anticipated consequences for Kim

Kim's original questions were:

◆ 'Where are we going wrong?'

◆ 'What should our next steps be?'

Our analysis of this has focused on the relationship between the players involved and on Kim and Carl's motivation. So far it feels like the project has fluctuated between painful progress and slow failure. Our hypothesis is that the relatively poor relationship between the players is a major contributing factor. When Kim and Carl have pushed, they have made progress, but they have not been able to sustain this drive as their frustrations at the lack of apparent progress have risen.

A final piece of analysis highlights some unpleasant potential consequences of Kim and Carl's choices.

In the angle we talked about looking at the whole system in complex situations. Often key factors interfere with each other and can create reinforcing or limiting forces.

This may be happening here. There is a possibility that the source of frustration for Kim and Carl lies in the poor relationships between people involved in the project. At the same time the quality of the relationships may be a result of the drive coming from Kim and Carl.

This is a simple system:

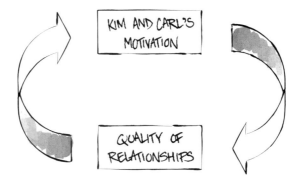

This is a reinforcing system. It suggests that poor relationships reduce motivation, which in turn reduces the quality of relationships. Alternatively, good relationships increase motivation and increase good relationships.

This will be part of a bigger system of forces at play. However it is an important, and possibly critical, sub-system because it will have the impact of amplifying either of the issues above and has the potential to drive either dimension quickly to an extreme.

The opportunity it presents is to find a way to invoke a positive cycle which could quickly turn the situation around.

It is through this type of systems thinking that you can best anticipate some of the consequences of choices. Not only what will happen, but also how quickly. So look for these sorts of reinforcing loops in complex situations.

So, what's your advice?

In the angle we pointed to the importance of keeping moving. Avoid getting stuck in the analysis. Work with the complexity, but work to the next step, maintain momentum.

Some of our analysis is quite crude. The systems map could be elaborated substantially. However, our objective here is to help make an important yet short-term decision, so we have kept our investment in analysis appropriate to that. Give appropriate time to thinking.

So between us, I imagine we have done enough to give Kim some advice. What would it be?

Write it down:

We're not going to offer a model answer. (If only!)

If you want to know what our advice would be, you can infer it from the direction of our analysis. We think there is a destructive loop in operation, whereby Kim and Carl's understandable determination to make the project a success produces a pushing approach in which relationships and shared understandings are not adequately developed. This results in slow progress, which fuels Kim and Carl's pushing, and so on.

This clearly isn't the whole story because the behaviour of the other players then serves to hold this negative loop in place rather than shift it into a positive direction. Our advice would focus on the need to build better relationships among all those involved and that process would undoubtedly require more face-to-face time and joint attention to good thinking. This may require something dramatic, perhaps a big meeting, to change the direction of the system.

The key point, however, is not whether one answer is better than another.

How could you tell except by comparing them both in action, and of course you can't do that. Life isn't a laboratory. For once it is not the 'answer' that is important but the process of thinking through the complexity and identifying choices and consequences. What is important is to pay attention to the process, because that's all we have to work with in 'real' time.

Footnote

There was no intervention from the outside at this point in the Networker story. You were not there for them.

On 22 August, after continuing difficulties in achieving agreement and progress within the project working group, Kim and Carl sent a letter of withdrawal to the Genesis Association board. The letter cited factors contributing to this decision, including *'unprofessional behaviour, lack of trust, fundamental changes of objectives, skewed research, misinformation and scaremongering'.*

So, was Networker a victim of politics?

politics

an angle on

politics

making sense of where they're coming from

You could say that politics in organizations is a special case of complexity. So why choose to give it focus as one of our five primary angles that we suggest will help you get clued up?

Firstly, politics acts as a good starting point for introducing a number of critical ideas about how to be effective in organizations. Politics is all about vested interests and that includes yours, what really matters to you, the things that will ultimately decide whether you want to work for an organization or not. Your values.

Secondly, politics has been viewed as somewhat of a taboo subject.

Something not to talk about openly in the staff restaurant, something slightly underhand and dirty. As a consequence it is probably not an area that you have been encouraged to think about or act on. Therefore there is something here about seeking to redress the balance, to ensure that one set of clues you do pick up to inform your choices is the political one.

David Butcher and Martin Clarke in their book *Smart Management* (Palgrave, 2001) define politics as 'those deliberate efforts made by individuals and groups in organizations to use power in pursuit of their own particular interests'. As this definition suggests, politics is inextricably linked with power, that is the ability to get others to do what they might not otherwise do.

Power is an interpersonal thing. Getting others to do things for you requires interaction. It potentially requires resolution of differences, dealing with conflict. Not only do you need to know what you want to get from a confrontation, but also you have to get your message across. Here we are moving from the idea side to the action side of the gap. Knowing what to do is necessary, but not sufficient. You also have to act effectively. How often have you been surprised by the impact of what you have said? The meaning of communication is the response you get.

The final angle focuses specifically on the words you use to put your ideas into action. In the knowledge economy words form a large part of what constitutes action and generally we do not give our choice of language sufficient attention. Under the heading of politics we will begin to look at interpersonal effectiveness as relationships lie at the heart of being effective in this domain.

The style of this angle differs from the previous ones. We flagged in the book's introduction that we would be asking you increasingly to engage with the material. Not only to be reflecting on the ideas presented, seeing them in the context of the Networker story, but critically thinking about your own circumstances. This angle contains a lot of questions. The aim is to encourage you to reflect on your own context. Some of you may do this as you go through, others may want to pass through all the material first and reflect at the end. Again, go with what works for you. The episode will take this further and ask you to think critically about a specific idea of yours.

Before getting into practicalities, there is a question we need to answer.

Politics, good or bad?

Well, unless this is your first chapter (which it might be, there is something strangely attractive about the subject matter), then I suspect you know our answer to this. Again it is not, for us, a matter of right or wrong. Politics just is. Placing a value judgement on it we believe is unhelpful. There are definitely actions that could be considered political, which may be more or less effective, depending on your viewpoint, but good or bad is too extreme.

Politics as a subject area does bring out extreme behaviour.

We had one person walk out of a workshop in their organization as they simply felt it a completely inappropriate topic for discussion. Ironically this action could itself be an example of naive political behaviour, but more of that later.

Perhaps the reason for this dramatic reaction is that politics is an area that most obviously challenges the rational, 'scientific' mindset discussed at the beginning of the previous angle. The idea that individuals should legitimately have vested interests and, furthermore, pursue them through the influencing of others does not fit the mechanical metaphor for organizations that we believe is so prevalent. What's more, without this dominant model the way those 'in charge' need to behave is challenged. With a political frame of reference people may choose not to 'follow orders' and the predictability of the organizational system breaks down.

So a political viewpoint can be seen to be challenging to the established order and thus potentially subversive. However, isn't it absurd not to think of people having an interest in the outcome of their work and effort? Actually, haven't the past few years in organizations been all about engaging staff in the activities of the business? In spite of this it seems that many managers would still like to believe that you can decide on a direction at the top of an organization, tell everyone what it is and then expect everyone to fall into line and follow. Or at least that is what their behaviour towards introducing change seems to suggest.

Let's face it. Politics and political behaviour are a natural consequence of any human system.

It is not that politics is wrong, but that it doesn't fit with the (limited) picture many people carry around as to how corporate life operates. If you are to be clued up then your picture of your world needs to be rich enough to encompass political behaviour.

Right, sermon over. On to more useful stuff.

So where is all this politics?

We are presenting political behaviour as a significant part of the idea-action gap, a major cause of complexity in organizations. If you are going to be clued up to it, where do you find political behaviour and what does it look like?

Gerard Egan identifies a number of key aspects of political activity in his book *Working the Shadow Side* (Jossey-Bass, 1994). Drawing from this we suggest that you:

1 *Observe behaviours in the vicinity of scarce, prized resources.* What is it that people really want in your organization and that is difficult to get hold of? Budget? Headcount? Office space? Time with the managing director? Who is successful at securing these? How do they go about it?

2 *Uncover the motivation underlying competitive activities.* Identify where competition is taking place, e.g. for desirable positions. Why is it happening? What are the views of each side? What has happened previously to influence the current situation?

3 *Identify the sources of power.* Identify who in your organization has influence over others. On what basis do they persuade people to do what they want? Where do they get their power? Who has control over

distribution of rewards and benefits? How are key decisions taken? Who sets policy?

4 *Observe the strategies of political players.* What do they do? Are there different types of political player? How do you feel about each of them? How do they protect their territory and empire?

Types of political behaviour

So if this is where we might find politics, what patterns of political behaviour might we encounter?

We have aimed to be sparing with conceptual models in this book. We suspect that many of you are already overloaded with different frameworks and tools. That is not to say having structured ways of organizing thoughts and ideas does not have a value. We are going to use one here, originated by writers Simon Baddeley and Kim James, initially to categorize types of political behaviour in a memorable way.

Political behaviour has two important facets.

1 The extent to which someone is aware of what is going on around them. In our language, how well do they spot the clues?

2 How open someone is in their intentions. Is it clear what motivations are behind their actions?

Presenting these as two axes, we get our organizer.

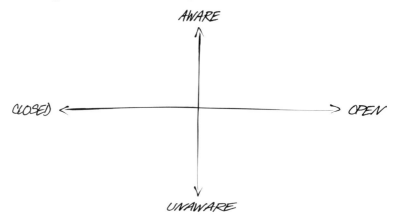

Now consider each quadrant. What types of behaviour might you expect to see in each? We return here to an old favourite from the last angle. If you were to think of an animal that represented the typical behaviour in each quadrant, what would it be?

Baddeley and James chose four memorable animals.

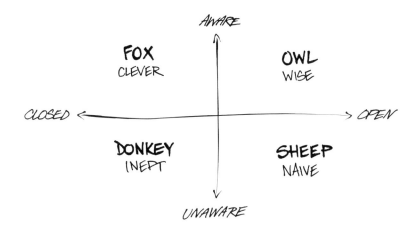

We have used this framework with many groups and people readily identify with each of these characters in their organizations. Can you recognize people you know filling these roles?

Where are you?

Are you in one quadrant all the time or do you find yourself adopting different positions as circumstances change?

If so, what influences the position you adopt? What about your key working relationships? How does their position impact the way you work together?

Organizers of this sort are also useful for thinking about the dynamics of a situation. That is, how political behaviour develops over time. As you think about these different roles, where do you think most people start when they are new to an organization? What trajectories have you seen develop?

Our experience suggests that many people start out as naive. Becoming aware of what is going on takes time and most people enter organizations with positive intentions, without interests to protect by being closed. We have plotted three common trajectories from there.

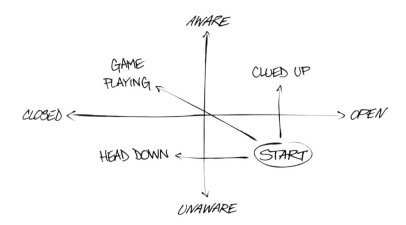

At first sight it may be hard to see why anyone would want to be anything other than clued up. Can you think of any time when you put your head down, kept your true intentions to yourself, didn't seek to find out what was really going on? If so, what went on immediately before the decision to follow that strategy? What were the consequences of that approach?

How about game playing? Surely as a momentum reader you don't do that kind of thing? Or are there times when it feels like you don't really have a choice? Can you recall a particular example? What was going on then?

Underlying these positions we see two important dilemmas. These may be reasons why being clued up in this political sense can be a hard position to maintain.

The first dilemma relates to the awareness dimension.

KEEPING UP TO DATE
WITH WHAT'S GOING
ON AROUND YOU TAKES
TIME AND MAY
DISTRACT YOU FROM
GETTING THE JOB DONE

FOCUSING ON THE JOB
MAY BE AT THE EXPENSE
OF KNOWING WHAT'S
GOING ON AROUND YOU

Delivery is a key attribute for most, if not all, of us in organizations. The 'rightsizing' process has generally left little slack in most businesses and everyone has to be on top of getting their job done. In this setting putting your head down may be a very legitimate approach, especially if you're under particular pressure to deliver. Unfortunately this may be self-defeating as effective delivery may require an awareness of what's going on.

So what can you do about it?

Well, it is partly about time management. Which incidentally we believe to be one of life's most misleading labels. How can you manage time, it is about the only constant thing there is these days! There are always 365 days a year, 24 hours a day, 60 minutes an hour. What you manage is priorities. Managing this dilemma is a priority in our view. Without awareness you are condemned to be a sheep or a donkey!

The second is a recurring theme in this book. Being clued up is about being alert in the moment, using what is already happening around you to inform you. It need not be a time-consuming activity. It also 'pays back'. A little time up front clarifying what's going on can mean a big saving in implementing your idea. In a similar way to giving thinking time, give time to building awareness.

For a moment we were tempted by the phrase, 'being clued up is a journey, not a destination', but fortunately this is being written on a Sunday morning and there is no tolerance for such a cheesy statement. (But you get the point, right?)

To be more practical, here are some suggestions for staying aware.

◆ Network.

◆ Cultivate informed sources of information.

◆ Prioritize your time on key relationships.

◆ Find mentors.

◆ Be a mentor.

◆ Get involved in cross-functional activities.

◆ Stay in touch with the grapevine.

◆ WATCH AND LISTEN.

◆ Ask questions.

The second dilemma, not surprisingly, refers to the openness dimension.

In essence this reflects a practical issue that it is not always possible to be open 100 per cent of the time. Others may take your openness and use the information it gives to their advantage and possibly your disadvantage. Also you may have information which is of a confidential nature that can not be shared in a completely open way. As a powerful person in an organization, people will come to you in confidence, 'Don't tell anyone, but…' However being closed, withholding what you know or your true intentions behind what you say or do, risks building distrust. This will impact your ability to get things done, it reduces your power. As we will discuss shortly, a number of the sources of power are based on relationships. It also diminishes your supply of information, as people do not share with you, uncertain of how you might use it. Your awareness suffers.

Trust is the key.

People accept the difficulties of organizational life. They will cut you some slack if there is an underlying confidence in your motives and intentions. Trust provides the elastic that allows you to manage your openness. This does not mean you can be a fox all the time, but it does allow you to stretch in that direction.

And how do you build trust?

Big question. One in which we need to avoid saying just that you need to be open! Our view is that there is a mix of ingredients that needs to be managed dynamically, from moment to moment. One of the reasons trust can be so elusive is that it requires good, consistent, 'real-time' performance. If we think of times when we have built trust in someone else, elements that have contributed probably include:

◆ openness;

◆ confidence in how they will behave;

◆ being treated fairly by them;

◆ being listened to and treated with respect;

◆ willingness to co-operate;

◆ keeping promises;

◆ when suspicion proves unfounded;

◆ when your own trust is not betrayed;

◆ when confidentiality is preserved;

◆ when these characteristics are consistent over time.

So far we have been setting the scene for politics. You should now have an idea about where to spot political behaviour, the patterns in which it emerges and some of the underpinning issues. However, as we are now firmly in the second half of this book we need to be nearer to action than ideas. The remainder of this angle therefore focuses on three key issues for your political effectiveness:

◆ your sources of power

◆ knowing what is important to you

◆ getting your point across.

Sources of power

As we mentioned earlier, politics and power are heavily intertwined. We defined power as the ability to get others to do things they wouldn't otherwise do. Therefore the amount of power you have is dependent on others and how they interpret you and your behaviour.

Think for a moment.

How much power do you have?

Is this with particular individuals or groups? Why?

What do you do when you exercise your power?

Understanding your sources of power and particularly how others see them is critical for effective action.

Rate yourself on this quick questionnaire.

Source of power over others	Rating	
	Low	**High**
Your position/authority	1 – 2 –③– 4 – 5	
Your control over resources/reward	1 – 2 – 3 –④– 5	
Ability for logical argument, persuasiveness	1 – 2 –③– 4 – 5	
Your dominance, assertiveness	1 –②– 3 – 4 – 5	
Your expertise	1 – 2 –③– 4 – 5	

Quality of your relationships:
obligations to you, number of connections   1 – 2 – 3 –④– 5
How attractive are you?
setting an example, inspiring others   1 – 2 –③– 4 – 5

What do the results say?

How confident in them are you?

How would others describe your power?

Do you have any extreme scores?

Do you overuse a strong source of power or miss opportunities because of a weak area?

You may well find that different sources of power work with different individuals or groups.

What about your key relationships? Map them out. What power do you have in relation to your boss? Where does it come from? How about your team or anyone to whom you give direction?

Can you identify particular patterns of power and influence in your organization? Are some sources used more than others? Is position dominant or is there a powerful informal network or something else? Are subject experts revered?

Sorry about all the questions, but it is important for you to reflect on this. Without a clear picture of your own influence, in the context of your organization, you are unlikely to be able to get that great idea successfully across the gap.

In thinking about these sources of power it is worth reflecting on the degree of influence you have over each of them. Increasing your position power, for example, is likely to be largely out of your control. That is not to say you shouldn't be seeking to influence others to effect this, but if this is your only strategy for increasing power then it is at best high risk.

The relationships you form, the expertise you build, the skills you develop to persuade others, these are things that are in your control.

Not totally – everything in this area relies on others, almost by definition – but substantially. Therefore work on the things that you think will have the biggest impact and over which you have a reasonable influence.

Pause at this point.

How does all this thought about power and politics make you feel? Emotions (or a lack of them) are often a big clue to what is going on for us. They are a way our unconscious brings important things to our attention. As we said, this has been a bit of a taboo subject so it would be quite natural to feel slightly uncomfortable with starting to consider you own power. Alternatively the feeling may be excitement – power can be quite a turn-on (or so we are told!) Whatever you are feeling, just be aware of it and carry on reading.

So what is really important?

To stay open and to use power effectively means you need to know where you are coming from. What are the things that are most important to you? These will provide an important guide in the uncertain territory of the gap. This sounds as if it ought to be easy, but often these things are so much part of our basic make-up that they are less obvious than you think.

These core values sometimes become clear only when we are facing important or difficult situations or decisions. Major dilemmas force us back to basics. Back to the fundamentals. Even then these decisions can remain unconscious. How often do you hear phrases like, 'It just felt right' or 'When I got there I knew what had to be done'?

We believe that raising your conscious understanding of these underpinning values will enable you to be more mindful in your political action.

So, write them down. What are the half a dozen most important things to you about your life and work?

Was that easy? Does the list feel right?

If you answered yes, then you probably have a reasonable grasp on what's important to you. Even so it is worth checking with some of the questions below. These will help if writing the list wasn't so easy. That is not to say you don't know what is important to you, more likely that those things are so embedded in what you do that you are not very aware of them.

Try some of these questions (sometimes having someone else asking them of you can help you think more clearly):

◆ What made you choose your current job?

◆ What do you like most/least about work at the moment? Why?

◆ What organizations would you refuse to work for? For what reasons?

◆ Think of the time you were most excited. What happened to give you this feeling? What was unique about this situation?

- When were you last really angry? What caused that?
- If there were only three things that you could have in life, what would they be?
- If you were shipwrecked on a desert island:
  - Who would you have as a companion? Why?
  - What three personal belongings would you want?
  - What would you most like to do with all the time you would have?

Pause and think about your answers. What themes do you see? What surprises you? How would you summarize the information? Now revisit your list of important things.

So, how is knowing this helpful?

Many of the assumptions we hold about the world have their roots in our values and beliefs.

These frames of reference in turn influence our behaviour. Being politically effective requires a conscious control over our behaviour. This is supported by an awareness of those things most important to us.

It is also when these values are 'under attack' that we often respond in an extreme way. This uncharacteristic behaviour can be detrimental to the trust others place in us.

Our aim here is to raise your awareness of those things that are important to you and help you become aware of what lies behind the decisions you take and the reactions you have. Part of being clued up is having awareness not only of what is going on outside but inside as well.

Given that you know where you are coming from, how do you make sure you can interact effectively to get that message across? How do you communicate successfully?

Getting your point across

Good intentions to be open are not enough. You also need to ensure that others recognize your behaviour as open. This can be more difficult than it seems, some of the reasons for which are rooted in basic human psychology.

As human beings we are designed to 'make sense' of the world going on around us. We are expert at seemingly knowing what is happening around us. The quantity and complexity of the data that our brains are processing is extreme, yet we are rarely caught out by situations that don't instantly make sense. When was the last time you entered a room and were taken aback by being unable to comprehend what was happening?

To enable us to cope our brain uses a number of processes which have important consequences for communication. First, over time we have developed a series of filters to interpret the raw data entering our head. At a simple level this allows us to recognize common objects, but these filters also become highly personalized, based on our unique set of experiences. Therefore none of us has the same experience of the same event, we simply 'see' different things.

Second, the brain deals in wholes – a part picture doesn't make sense, so we automatically fill in the blanks. We have all experienced optical illusions, tricks that fool our minds. These are going on all the time, as we automatically assume data into areas where it is missing and without which the picture isn't whole.

This is particularly true in the political domain. Here we are dealing with imprecise intentions and motives which leads to substantial second-guessing, both conscious and unconscious.

It also makes one of the most natural human activities – communicating to each other – a lot tougher than it might at first appear. There is always a difference between the message intended and that received: the arc of distortion.

Getting a sense of the size of the arc is doubly difficult because you can only judge your communication based on the response you get.

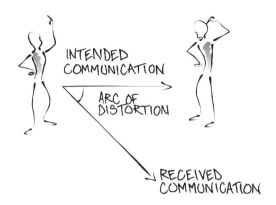

INTENDED COMMUNICATION

ARC OF DISTORTION

RECEIVED COMMUNICATION

It too is subject to distortion as your filters interpret the intended response.

This communication is not just what you say. In fact, if you believe the research, the interpretation of meaning in communication has little to do with the actual words. In face-to-face conversation meaning is communicated:

- 7 per cent from the words you use;

- 28 per cent from your tone of voice;

- 65 per cent from your physiology or body language.

This is not to say that the words you use are not vital. In fact, we will be devoting a whole angle to them shortly. The way in which you use words, however, provides the context in which others interpret them.

Often we are not consciously controlling our physiology (when communicating, that is!), so it is often what we unconsciously believe that is communicated through body language. This is why we are much more effective at getting our message across if we believe in it. If we don't or if we are talking about something that conflicts with what we believe, our body gives it away. Just think of the last person who said to you, 'Oh, I'm fine' and you knew they were anything but okay (head bowed, quiver in the voice, avoiding eye contact, and so on).

What we are saying is that a carefully crafted set of words will not get the message across unless they are in synch with your voice and body.

The best way to do this is to be open in what you believe about a subject.

This also helps explain our natural intuition that difficult messages are best handled face to face. Put the other way round, e-mail (i.e. words only) is a very difficult way to communicate meaning. What is worse, the reader applies their own choice of tonality when reading it. The 'arc of distortion' can be very large with e-mail.

So what can I do about this?

First, in listening to others be attentive to all the methods of communication. This will give you a better understanding of their true meaning. Likewise for your communication. Be aware.

Use good communication skills. Ask questions to check meaning. Keep it simple. Don't make assumptions.

Ask for feedback. The better understanding you have of how others see you, the more likely you are to communicate effectively. You need to uncover your 'blind spots', the things others see but you don't.

Giving feedback is tough (as is receiving it). A good way to encourage others to give feedback is to offer something about you that they may not know. Disclose how you are feeling, for example. This obviously needs to be appropriate to the situation you are in. Suddenly offering the managing director the details of your criminal record is unlikely to lead to a quality response.

This sort of exchange, disclosure and feedback opens up the understanding you share with someone and will improve relationships as well as communication.

How much do you share about yourself?

With whom? Does it differ between boss, peers, team? Why?

How much do you know about those around you?

Is there a balance between what you know of them and what they know of you?

Acting effectively in a political environment means being in control of your impact on others. To do that you have to know how others see you, which relies on effective communication. Being open will encourage others to respond in an open way and will build trust.

So what have we learned?

All organizations are political. Some are more closed and manipulated than others. They have more foxes and donkeys. Being a wise player means being clued up. It means knowing what is going on in your business, with your boss, at this moment in your interaction, and most fundamentally in yourself.

We have moved further through the gap with this angle. Our focus has been more on action than ideas. The focus has been on communication and particularly being effective in getting your message across. These are skills and as such hard to develop through a book. However, there is an attitude of mind that we hope to have influenced. It's all about attention. Paying attention to others. Paying attention to you.

Ideas and action both happen through words. Our thinking relies on words, as do our interactions with others. The words other people use and the way they use them provide a rich source of clues.

Our last angle and episode looks at how to use talk effectively. Before that an episode on politics which will help you to explore your own situation in much greater depth.

an episode on
politics

Now it is over to you.

In this chapter we will be using some material from Networker, but the primary focus will be on you working on your own material.

Our aim throughout this book has been to increase your awareness. To help you spot the clues that are around you and thereby make more informed choices about your actions. We have avoided introducing a plethora of new models, tools or stepwise guides to success. Life is lived in the moment, therefore what is most useful is what you can hold in your head so that you can use it when it is needed.

Stuff that is in your head is not necessarily conscious. We have talked a number of times about the power of the unconscious mind. Our conscious is limited and its attention is ever being drawn from one thing to another.

Being effective in the moment therefore relies substantially on your unconscious capabilities.

Sounds odd, but if you think of how you act moment to moment, much goes on without you apparently 'thinking about it'. In other words it happens out of your conscious, that is unconsciously.

So, what has this got to do with this episode?

Well, there is a need to embed the ideas from the chapter in your unconscious so that they are ready for when you need them. One way to do this is through practice.

If you have ever learned a sport, you'll remember how many things there seemed to be to remember to start with. How to hold the racket, how to swing your arm, what to pay attention to, and so on. As you practise, many of these things start to happen 'naturally'. That is the aim here.

This may seem an elaborate justification for why you should do some of the work now. We suspect that many of you will be tempted to skip this bit, or perhaps use those immortal words, 'I'll come back to this later'. We think you'll miss something if you do, however tempting it may seem.

The previous episode, on complexity, was about conducting a broad analysis of the idea-action gap. The approach was to map the key factors in order to make sense of them, so that a direction for action could be chosen. The nature of the work in this episode is different. This is about deep analysis to enable specific personal actions to be planned. We are going to ask you to work through the models from the politics angle and start the process of building an influencing strategy.

So where do I start?

Decide on the three most critical individuals for you at work. Criticality is subjective and will vary over time. We suggest you think of the most important things going on for you right now and select your three accordingly. (There is nothing magical about the number three, but it will give you sufficient complexity to work with, without creating an overwhelming task.)

If these three are not obvious to you, maybe your world is too complex, then follow some of the advice in the complexity angle. Do a map. The procedure described in the complexity episode for mapping would work here.

Where does the power lie?

Take each of your three in turn and complete the questionnaire on the next page (taken from the previous angle).

Person 1 _____

Source of power over others	Rating	
	High	**Low**
Their position/authority	1 – 2 – 3 – 4 – 5	
Their control over resources/reward	1 – 2 – 3 – 4 – 5	
Ability for logical argument, persuasiveness	1 – 2 – 3 – 4 – 5	
Their dominance, assertiveness	1 – 2 – 3 – 4 – 5	
Their expertise	1 – 2 – 3 – 4 – 5	
Quality of their relationships:		
obligations to them, number of connections	1 – 2 – 3 – 4 – 5	
How attractive are they?		
setting an example, inspiring others	1 – 2 – 3 – 4 – 5	

Person 2 _____

Source of power over others	Rating	
	High	**Low**
Their position/authority	1 – 2 – 3 – 4 – 5	
Their control over resources/reward	1 – 2 – 3 – 4 – 5	
Ability for logical argument, persuasiveness	1 – 2 – 3 – 4 – 5	
Their dominance, assertiveness	1 – 2 – 3 – 4 – 5	
Their expertise	1 – 2 – 3 – 4 – 5	
Quality of their relationships:		
obligations to them, number of connections	1 – 2 – 3 – 4 – 5	
How attractive are they?		
setting an example, inspiring others	1 – 2 – 3 – 4 – 5	

Person 3 _____

Source of power over others	Rating	
	High	**Low**
Their position/authority	1 – 2 – 3 – 4 – 5	
Their control over resources/reward	1 – 2 – 3 – 4 – 5	
Ability for logical argument, persuasiveness	1 – 2 – 3 – 4 – 5	
Their dominance, assertiveness	1 – 2 – 3 – 4 – 5	
Their expertise	1 – 2 – 3 – 4 – 5	
Quality of their relationships:		
obligations to them, number of connections	1 – 2 – 3 – 4 – 5	
How attractive are they?		
setting an example, inspiring others	1 – 2 – 3 – 4 – 5	

Stand back and look at the results.

What do they tell you?

Can you see any patterns?

What is the relative power among the three? If you were to rank them, what order would they come in?

How dependent is each person on the situation they are in for their power? Is their power consistent across situations? If not, what are the variables with which it alters?

How powerful are they in relation to you? If you wanted to increase your power relative to each one of them, what specific actions would you need to take? What would get in the way of you taking such actions?

This should start to build up a picture of the relative power of these key individuals and their sources of power. Having a good awareness of this will help you decide who to influence and how, when you come to plan any actions.

It is important not only to consider these people as individuals but also to recognize where they fit within the political systems of their organization(s).

What does politics look like around here? (Have another look at the second Networker episode if you want some ideas. We haven't pulled out examples because you need to see them in context. It will also be good clue-spotting practice!)

In the angle on politics we suggested four areas in which you could observe political behaviour most easily. Think about each for the organization(s) of your key people:

Behaviours in the vicinity of scarce, prized resources.

The motivation underlying competitive activities.

The sources of power.

The strategies of political players.

You now need to bring together the data on the organization(s) with that of your key individuals.

How do your individuals fare relative to those things most important in their organization? Do they do better or worse than is typical? Why?

What do you know about their underlying motives? If you are unsure, what might you suppose from their behaviour?

What sort of successful strategies have you observed? Are these used by any of your key three people? Do you use any of these strategies?

What are the patterns of behaviour?

Thinking about strategies that are used leads us nicely into overall patterns of political behaviour.

As you think about each of your three key players, would you categorize them as:

	Person 1	Person 2	Person 3
a) Owl			
b) Fox			
c) Donkey			
d) Sheep			

Often our gut instincts are right. Reflect on why you categorized each in this way.

Now collect your thoughts. Here are some questions to help you.

◆ Do the animals chosen correspond to the behaviour you see from each of your key people on the awareness dimension and on the openness dimension?

◆ What do each of the people do to maintain their awareness? How many of these tactics do you use?

◆ In what situations do you see each person display closed behaviours? How does this impact on your trust of them?

◆ How would you characterize your own behaviour (honestly)? What prevents you putting more time into developing your awareness? Do your key players trust you? How do you know?

The questions you can ask around these areas are almost endless (and may feel it!). If you have managed to give most of these some thought, you should by now be developing a good sense of the political arena in which you are operating with respect to your key individuals.

How do you make use of this analysis?

What you have done so far is to describe the general political context in which your ideas or actions will have to survive. Therefore, in using your increased awareness, you first need to be clear about the idea that you want to turn into action. In selecting your three important individuals, you may well already have had a clearly formed idea. If not, now is a time for some good thinking! These questions may help.

What is your idea? How would you describe it simply?

What are your specific objectives in relation to the three individuals identified earlier?

How will you know that you have been successful?

Right. Now think about the political context into which you will plunge your idea.

Who will be a supporter, an advocate, for the idea? How powerful are they? Does your idea play to their political strengths?

How about anyone who might not support the idea? How will this impact them?

Is there anyone who might support you in this who will not be directly affected by the idea? What is in it for them?

These questions have been leading us into developing an influencing strategy. As with other complex processes, developing a map of the territory can help distinguish appropriate strategies to be influential. There are many good books written on the tactics of influencing and 'stakeholder' management, so we will be brief here. The following map is one that we, and those we have worked with, have found useful.

As you'll see it proposes different strategies depending on the attitude of the person or people you are looking to influence and their degree of influence. For example, it suggests that if someone is a 'fence-sitter' and without influence, you should not be using up limited time and energy on them now. Perhaps keep an eye on them to see if they shift. In a world where these two things are often our scarcest resources, deciding who to leave alone is important.

Where would you focus your energy?

Here's a way of picturing the choices.

ADVOCATE	'WORTHLESS FRIENDS'	BEST FRIENDS
'FENCE-SITTER'	LONG-TERM PROSPECTS	IMMEDIATE PROSPECTS
OPPONENT	THREATS	DANGEROUS ENEMIES
	WITHOUT INFLUENCE	WITH INFLUENCE

The language is a bit provocative here. 'Worthless friends.' We've used it for effect, to make the clues louder. The point we're making is that they're potentially worthless in this context, not as friends in general.

Where would you focus your energy?

We think the answer lies back with the type of analysis you have been carrying out on your three individuals. If you have a good political understanding, and awareness of their motives and power sources, you should be able to find a way to turn a fence-sitter into an advocate. Therefore we propose under these circumstances to go for the influential fence-sitter. The tendency is to build coalitions with your supporters, regardless of their degree of influence. A more comfortable option often, but the challenge of building influence may well be greater than persuading one fence-sitter about your idea.

We can add the main influencing tactics to our picture.

	WITHOUT INFLUENCE	WITH INFLUENCE
ADVOCATE	'WORTHLESS FRIENDS' WORK TOGETHER ——→	BEST FRIENDS
		CONVINCE
'FENCE-SITTER'	LONG-TERM PROSPECTS (KEEP YOUR EYE ON)	IMMEDIATE PROSPECTS
OPPONENT	THREATS	DANGEROUS ENEMIES
	←—— DISTRACT	

Where do your three individuals sit?

What approaches could you take to move them up and to the right?

Okay. Probably a good point to scan back over your notes and summarize what you have learned about your individuals in relation to your idea. Focus particularly on any concrete actions you are now going to take.

So that's politics then.

Well, that would be too easy. Too many books or training programmes stop at this point. But not if you're clued up.

The above analysis, rational as it may appear, glosses over two vital processes for the person with momentum.

Firstly, how do you know if someone is for or against your idea. Sounds easy, but in our complex world this is rarely straightforward. Secondly, once you have done all this analysis you have to be able to act on it, to be effective in what could potentially be difficult conversations.

How do you know if someone is for or against your idea?

In the black-and-white world it is simple, they tell you. Is this a good idea, yes or no?

In the messiness of modern life things are more subtle.

For a start your idea is likely to have many facets, reducing the relevance of yes or no. It is context that is vital to appreciate here. People's apparent support, or otherwise, will be based on their understanding of the context in which they see your idea, at any moment in time. As their understanding of context develops, or simply changes, so may their support for your idea. It's like with personal effectiveness, there's a tendency to attribute the support to the individual and ignore context.

The burden of constantly checking everyone's position prevents this being a viable strategy, so you need to develop a more general sense of where your key players 'are coming from'. This general understanding, part of what we have earlier referred to as awareness, can then be applied to specific situations as they unfold. You develop a sense of how key people will react.

Hmm…

So how do you do that then?

Back to spotting clues again.

People are constantly telling us about themselves. The way in which they speak, what they choose to comment on, what they get passionate about and so on, all provide a window on what they value and believe in. You need to watch, listen and build a picture of where people are coming from.

This is a process we unconsciously undertake all the time. How often after a first meeting do you have a sense of liking or disliking someone? (And how often does it turn out to be wrong!) Again we are suggesting you become more aware of this evaluation activity so that you can guide it and use it more carefully.

This comes with practice. To give you a go at spotting clues we want to introduce a new character, Saheena, from the Networker story. You may have spotted her as part of the project sub-group.

Below is a small part of her description of her involvement in the project. All she is doing is responding to the request to tell the story from her point of view. In doing so, however, she also tells us about herself. See what you can spot. Focus on what you can infer about her general views or situation rather than follow the story that she is telling.

I kinda knew what Kim was doing when she came back from her travels, when she had done her arm. So I knew her thoughts were in terms of this website. I knew she had been talking to Malcolm about that and she had been sending through quite a bit of stuff to me, in terms of how they wanted to sort data on the website and that kinda stuff.

And as much as I ever can, because I've got a lot of stuff going on, I would sort of feed her back bits and pieces, but that was all my input was at a really early stage. When we went to the conference – actually no, it was just before the conference which was back in June time – Kim mentioned to me about...well, she told me she had been having conversations with Mattie about her joining the board and she suggested to me why didn't I join the board as well.

Ermm, and I wasn't that keen, but having said that I had been quite involved with getting one of the speakers for the conference and I...actually from my point of view I thought it would be a good way of building some bridges with Mattie because I haven't actually got on dreadfully well with her in the past.

There was an issue on the programme to do with placements. Well she would get paid for getting me a placement, but she got me one which I didn't actually want, but somebody else wanted it. I then got interviewed by the company that I still work for. I knew that I had to work for that MD and took that job instead and she went up in arms and for a period of three or four years after that whenever I saw Mattie you knew that she didn't approve of what I did, even though somebody else took the placement and she got the money so she didn't lose anything, but she didn't like the fact that I hadn't taken the job, but it wasn't right for me so I had to go with what was right. Anyway, that was where we had come from.

So I thought it would help build the relationship with her and also because I was going to go into business then it would be good networking, so all right, I'll think about it, and I told Mattie that I would do it.

During the time before the voting for the people at the conference, Kim said to me something about she had had a meeting with the rest of the board the night before and she had actually started to see the light in terms of getting through to them, but she needed to, ermm, get some support in terms of getting things through and I suppose I should have twigged slightly what she was implying, but you know, it went straight over my head.

In the bar that night Kim came up to me and said they were going to have a steering group for the Networker project and I think you should volunteer to be on it. I didn't really want to volunteer, because I was starting to feel a bit uncomfortable about it, but, sorry, I tend to say yes.

So what do you know about Saheena after a few minutes listening to her. Scribble down some thoughts:

We learn some factual things:

◆ She knows Kim, Mattie and Malcolm.

◆ She was on the programme.

◆ She got her current job while on the programme.

◆ She is thinking of going into business for herself.

But there is much more we can infer about her as an individual.

◆ Saheena is someone who is able to make up her mind quickly, particularly when influenced by other people. (Her decision on a placement on meeting the MD.)

◆ She is sensitive to relationships around her. (Concerns about the relationship with Mattie.)

◆ She doesn't always act on her instincts, perhaps saying yes when she would rather say no. (Her discomfort in agreeing with Kim to join the steering group.)

◆ In spite of being busy she is willing to help where she can. (Providing feedback to Kim in the early days of the project.)

◆ Possibly an issue in handling conflict. (Inferred from the last two points, but needs verification with more information.)

Now this analysis is based on inferences from a very small amount of data but is intended to illustrate the amount of information that is available in what we say and how we say it. This builds a rich picture and should help you to decide whether someone will be for or against your idea.

Why did Kim encourage Saheena to join the steering group?

Perhaps she felt the group would benefit from Saheena's experience, intellect and objectivity. However, the overture is interpreted by Saheena as political, which is something she seems to be uncomfortable with. Is this a reaction that Kim has considered or was she just looking for a familiar face?

> I got an inkling that she wanted me there for a reason. She wanted me there to be on her side.

From this perspective Kim could appear to be enlisting Saheena as a supporter looking to build a coalition with her. This is in line with our influencing chart. Saheena, as a new member to the board, will probably start with low influence, therefore placing her in the top left of the chart.

But Saheena's interpretation of Kim's approach as political then has other consequences.

> Now unfortunately for me, or unfortunately for Kim and unfortunately for me because I never actually said to her, if I am in an official position I take that official position very seriously. I am there to serve the board in the interest of the members and if that is the role that I have taken on then I have to be…I can't afford to have any biases in that, otherwise what's the point of doing it. And I should have said to her no and I didn't and I just said fair enough.

So how does this leave Saheena disposed towards Kim's project? Advocate? Fence-sitter? Opponent? Try placing her on our influencing map. At best she sounds neutral and, unless she builds early influence, is going to be someone Kim might be best advised to leave alone, in terms of influencing strategy. This area will almost always demand deep thinking.

That was the first concern with the approach to influencing. The second concern related to the activity of 'convincing'. Having done all the analysis, understood the situation, identified your influential individual, now all you have to do is win them over.

This all sounds fine and dandy. But get real. It is a hostile environment out there, full of conflict and disagreement.

How do you deal with the difficult conversations?

In our experience it is common for people to dislike conflict and they find it hard to deal with. Many of us fall into familiar routines for handling disagreements. These habits, as we have said before, limit our choices, reduce our flexibility, make us less effective. Worry about the interchange can lead us to be less open and as such prevent us acting in a politically effective manner.

So what is conflict? In essence it is the battle between what you want and what somebody else wants, when those wants differ. If we think of our behaviour in conflict, we are finding ways to balance these two interests, our opponent's and ours.

If we can maintain our open behaviour and encourage the other person to do likewise, then there is a chance of collaborating. This collaboration could find a new solution to the problem you are facing that meets both sets of needs. We strongly recommend this as your entry approach. Make this your normal starting point because it is a win-win strategy.

It takes time and often courage, but it has big benefits.

Other ways of approaching conflict have a role to play, however. Just as with political behaviour there is a need for flexibility. You need to have choices.

There will be times when avoiding conflict will be important. Perhaps where you know that the disagreement will become a distraction from the important work at hand or where emotions need to be allowed to cool off before a considered discussion can take place.

But beware. Constructing what is going on simply so that you can avoid an uncomfortable conversation is unlikely to be effective. It is important to see the situation in as objective a way as possible.

Sometimes conceding your wants in favour of the other person's will be effective, perhaps where overall harmony is paramount or where the maintenance of the relationship needs to take priority.

You may not find conflict difficult. You may be willing to argue your case come what may.

Do you really think you can be right all the time? Do you risk missing the value in the counter argument through your urge to win? A confrontational style can be very powerful in the moment, but often has 'downstream' consequences and probably needs to be used sparingly.

One common way to approach conflict is to seek compromise. This is often effective when a quick solution is required. Each side gives a bit but gets something of what they want. This will rarely reach the quality of solution that collaboration could provide.

Okay, those are the principles, but where are you? And where are you in the sort of situation you've been working on in this episode? If you want to explore that question more deeply, you need to think about your actual behaviour in specific situations. We've provided a framework to help you with this at the end of the book.

The appendix contains a short questionnaire that we have developed for this book. It builds on a well-used framework created by Ken Thomas and Ralph Kilmann. It will help you think about your habitual approaches to handling conflict and the impact of the different contexts in which you operate.

If you think you are someone who sometimes doesn't get all they want from situations involving conflict (and that is probably most of us!), then give it a go.

Meanwhile, going back to your own situation, what exactly are you going to say to your three key people?

Which brings us to our final angle.

politics

clued up

momentum

talking action

an angle on
talking action
the words that make things happen

Do your words make things happen? That's the test of whether they are effective. So this is a chapter about the power of words or wordpower, which we believe to be one of the most neglected, yet most potent, angles in being personally effective. But don't worry. This isn't going to be a lesson in grammar or a test of your spelling. What we're interested in are words in action, real speech in real situations, and what makes them work or fail.

We're going to look at why words matter, and when they matter in particular.

We're going to draw your attention to some of the most common shortcomings in the way we use language, and the consequences of these. And, most importantly, we're going to suggest what effective wordpower sounds like and how you can develop your ability to make things happen with words.

Here's a word of caution. There's a limit to how much wordpower you can have by yourself. You can learn about it privately, although that's not necessarily the best way. You can even develop it to some extent privately. But wordpower is only ever tested – and proven – in interaction with others. So most of what we say is going to be about dialogue and action through dialogue.

Right, to work.

Why language is so important

You may recall the story of the Tower of Babel. It tells how the ancient Babylonians, wanting to make a name for themselves, set out to build a tower so tall that its top would reach to heaven, and how God's response to this presumption was to bring the proceedings to an abrupt halt by confusing the workers' language so that they could no longer understand each other. It's an interesting story because it recognizes that when everyone is speaking the same language, there is potentially no limit to what can be achieved.

It's common to dismiss words as being the opposite of action. 'We don't want this to be a talking shop.' But, in the modern occupational and organizational context, words are our primary means of action. Words are what we use to get things done. We manage with our tongues rather than our hands. Think about it. Most of us spend a huge proportion of our day working with words, whether words on paper, characters on a screen, or words spoken in talking aloud and listening to others. That's where the action is. Even in extreme situations, when we're disagreeing with each other, arguing, fighting our corner, that's how we do it these days. You don't see much arm-wrestling in meetings, but you do hear plenty of 'verbal'.

The problem is not that words are short of action but rather that we are not as good as we could be, as we need to be, with our use of words. We tend to be short of wordpower.

Words have power because they shape the way people think and behave. So if we want to be influential and persuasive, then we'd better make sure we have the wordpower for it.

But even before we turn to the question of how we can come up with powerful utterances, there's a prior issue that we need to recognize.

Because, as we've pointed out already throughout this book, our actions don't take place in a vacuum. They happen in a context, and we need to make sense of that context if we are to be effective in it.

What form does the action take in that context? The form of words. And if words are where the action is, where are the clues? Embedded in the words. Embedded in the stream of words, sometimes easy to pick up, at other times much harder because they are partially hidden or obscured. That's why we admire people who are able to 'read between the lines'.

Because of course the action isn't just in the words themselves. It's also in the way we deliver the words. The action is in the language in the broadest sense. Remember those statistics that we cited in the previous angle about how much of the message is conveyed – or bound up – in the body language and the tonal accompaniment to the words. These figures suggest that only 7 per cent of the meaning is conveyed by the words themselves.

This might lead you to the conclusion that the words are comparatively unimportant, but that is patently absurd.

Just try going to your boss and seeking to deliver your next progress report or to answer her questions solely through a mixture of physical gestures and tonal variations. Then observe her reaction. That should illustrate how important the words are!

The real significance that body language and tone have for meaning is in highlighting the importance of context, and in particular the prevalence of 'noise' in the context surrounding the message of the words. We need to pay attention to these things because they provide clues about the ways in which the message is being muted, modified or masked.

Which brings us to a key point. Language is our medium of interaction. Words in themselves are inert. Sure, there may be some value in giving ourselves a good talking to from time to time. And there is certainly value in using words to enrich our thinking. We'll come back to that. But for the most part words acquire their power when they pass from one person to another.

Why are you reading this book? Why are you taking the time and the trouble to get to grips with 50,000 words? Because you want something from them. You expect them to do something. You want them to make a difference. You want them to enable you to think differently and be able to do at least some things that you couldn't do before.

That's certainly what we're trying to get them to do.

So we want our words to be movers and shakers. That's non-contentious in the case of this book. You chose to pick it up. Whether or not we succeed in giving you what you wanted, at least our intentions are aligned. But we also want our words to be movers and shakers, influential and persuasive, in those situations where others might not have come to the party so willingly. When we're arguing about what happened and why, or what the problem is and where, or who is responsible. When proposals are being pushed and resisted, when opinions are being aired, when judgements are being made. When courses of action are being discussed or disputed, when negotiations of all sorts are taking place.

Because this is the point: very little of our organizational lives is uncontested. That's a central feature of the messiness, this politics and complexity. We all have our own points of view and, increasingly, we're either expected or expect to be able to make that point of view known. Call it the age of the knowledge worker if you like, the bottom line is that we live and work in a world where there are many competing points of view and we need to be able to get ours across.

Getting our ideas across. Sounds like the idea-action gap again, doesn't it?

When do our words matter particularly?

Think about that question for a moment. When are our words particularly important? They don't matter so much all the time. In casual conversation our words are often decidedly 'dressed down'. Listen to the patterns of speech in informal discussion. Listen for instance to how seldom people speak in complete sentences.

Listen to how many utterances are single words or phrases, adding to or modifying what's already been said. Listen to how much remains unsaid, how much is inferred from what has gone before, including things that have gone long before in previous conversations. The edifice we call conversation is full of holes, a Tower of Babel indeed!

Now most of the time this doesn't matter very much. A conversation is just another chapter in an ongoing relationship, and if that relationship is close and has a lot of shared understanding, then there's less that needs to be said. But at other times, where the relationship is newer, or less open, or not as close, perhaps where interests are perceived to be more varied or simply not yet understood, we need to create our conversations more carefully. If we are to build understanding rather than misunderstanding, we need to choose and shape our materials, and above all our words, with greater care.

So when might our words matter a great deal? Here are some suggestions:

◆ When the issues we're dealing with are new, complex or unfamiliar.

◆ When an idea has to be pursued over a long period of time.

◆ When circumstances change or keep changing.

◆ When other people need to be persuaded.

◆ When these people are apprehensive or resistant.

◆ When we're finding it difficult to make sense of what's going on.

◆ When people don't seem to hear what we're trying to say.

This list may look familiar. It should do. It's pretty similar to one we put forward in our first angle about when ideas and projects tend to fall into the idea-action gap. But you'll recognize other themes in the list too: complexity and politics and situations where thinking needs to be good. These are all situations where being careless, or not careful enough, about what we're saying, and how we say it, often lies at the root of being personally ineffective. Being careful means paying attention to the particular situation, to the context, to the clues.

Try this little experiment, drawing from your experience.

Think about a difficult or challenging conversation that you've had recently, one that you knew was going to be difficult and that you were not looking forward to having.

Got one?

Okay, now bring to mind the issue or issues that you wanted to raise with the other person.

And then recall the issue or issues that they brought up with you.

How was the discussion? Well, we know it was difficult or challenging because you chose your example for that reason. But how did it feel? Uncomfortable? Awkward? Out of control? Frustrating? Infuriating?

Now ask yourself this. In preparing for that difficult discussion did you take the time to prepare what you were going to say? In particular, did you take the time and trouble to think through, even to write out, the first few sentences you were going to utter? Because these are crucial. These are the ones that introduce your issue and shape the tone for the encounter that is to follow.

We use this exercise frequently when we're coaching people on how to handle difficult discussions, such as performance reviews and feedback. Typically we use it as a preparation exercise, in anticipation of the difficult conversation. And almost every time we use it, we get the same reaction. Asked to write out what they're going to say, people's immediate response is to groan and exclaim, 'But that's difficult!'

Exactly.

But if it's difficult to be clear and precise about what we intend to say when we're preparing in our own time, how much harder is it to find the right words when we're face to face with the other person, amid the tension of the moment?

So what happens in your case? When you have important things to say, do you prepare with care? Do you invest in good thinking for those important occasions? Or do you do what so many people do, which is to put off thinking about it, get an approximate idea of what you're going to say, and trust that you'll be able to 'wing it' when the moment comes?

There's reason to believe that effective talking is even more challenging to achieve than good thinking.

The reason is to do with control.

First, good thinking, at least while we are thinking to ourselves, is within our own control. We have a better chance of managing it because it's going on in our heads, which can give it some protection from the noise and messiness which occurs when interacting with others. The management of a conversation, on the other hand, is shared, or more accurately negotiated, between us. Direction, pace, content and style are, to a greater or lesser extent, being contested from moment to moment, in the moment, throughout any conversation that we have. No wonder it's messy. No wonder it's difficult to use talking to do what we want.

Preparation can only be part of the answer. We can prepare for the start of our conversations. We can think carefully beforehand about what we want to say, how we want to say it, what sort of different reactions we might get, and how we might respond to each of those possibilities. But we can't anticipate everything. We have quite a lot of control over the launch of the proceedings, but after that the system we call conversation very rapidly becomes much more dynamic, complex and difficult to control.

How can we manage this challenge in the moment?

Once again, having a framework helps. It can provide no guarantees, but we can improve the odds. It gives us a map which can help us keep track of where we are moment to moment.

Like the other models in this book we've tried to keep it simple, memory-sized, so that you can retrieve it easily in the moment. Basically it provides a repertoire of three conversational moves. But to get to that simplicity, and show how you can connect it to what's going on in the moment, we have to build up the explanation one step at a time.

If we didn't have to worry about other people's opinions and interests, life would be so straightforward.

If we felt clued up, sure of what was going on around us, we could simply go ahead and act. If we felt unsure, we could investigate first.

I FEEL SURE ABOUT WHAT'S GOING ON,
AND I'M READY TO ACT

I FEEL UNSURE, SO I FIND OUT

But we do have to think about other people's views and interests, their attempts to influence our views and our need to influence theirs. So there's another dimension in the territory that we need to consider. Do we agree or disagree with them?

I DISAGREE
WITH YOU $\longleftarrow$ $\longrightarrow$ I AGREE
WITH YOU

In practice, of course, we often have to deal with both these dimensions at the same time, so in effect the territory for our interaction looks like this.

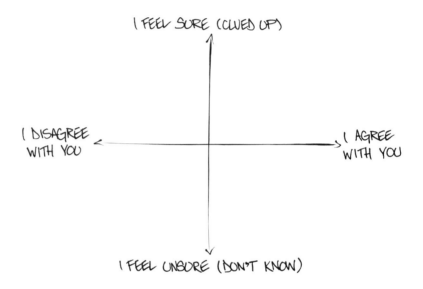

I FEEL SURE (CLUED UP)

I DISAGREE
WITH YOU

I AGREE
WITH YOU

I FEEL UNSURE (DON'T KNOW)

Think about this conversational territory for a minute.

Some of the areas of the grid seem more likely to occur than others. For instance, it should be easier for me to decide whether I agree or disagree with you if I'm feeling sure about what's going on. To put it another way, the further away we are from being sure about what's going on, the further away we should be from committing ourselves to either agreeing or disagreeing.

Therefore there are parts of this territory that are relatively safe, easier to navigate than others. And parts you would be crazy to entertain – agreeing, or even disagreeing, with someone when we have no idea what is going on (none of us does that now, do we!). Other parts are risky, but possible. Solid ground comes when you are clued up. This is when you can confidently make choices. This is best shown mapped to our grid.

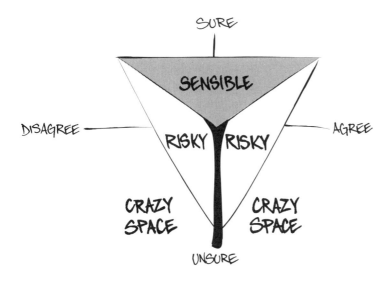

One of the advantages of this little framing device is that it's very easy to use. Essentially we only have to ask ourselves two questions to get a sense of where we are:

1   How sure do I feel about what's going on?

2   Do I agree with what you're saying?

These won't always yield exact answers, but they will usually provide ready ones, reasonable rules of thumb that we can access easily in the moment.

Types of conversation

So how do we use this?

Well, depending on the answer to these two questions, we will know which part of the territory we are in. What will we find there?

The grid points to three most likely areas, represented by the points of the triangle. Here we will find particular types of conversation and when each is appropriate.

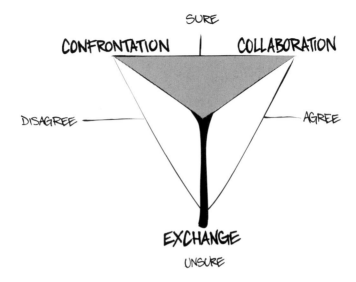

In other words, when I'm sure about what's going on but I disagree with you, we're heading for a confrontation. When I'm sure and I agree with you, we have the basis of a collaboration. When I'm feeling unsure, what's needed is an exchange.

By confrontation we mean the sort of conversation in which we are unwilling to take on, and sometimes even to consider, each other's point of view. We won't necessarily be openly angry, and we might even give each other the opportunity to speak (though probably not without interruption). Essentially the interaction is a battle of words, often characterized by each of us continuing to reassert our own particular perspective. It is a contest for control. The most obvious clue to this sort of talk is the sheer lack of movement, not physical but mental.

An exchange is the sort of conversation in which we are not only more willing to give each other a hearing but we take more trouble to understand each other's point of view. We may not necessarily agree with each other, and are often critical of what the other person has to say, but this is done constructively. We respect each other as independent thinkers. We offer challenges and expect to receive them. This is a recognition of autonomy. Perhaps the most obvious clue to this sort of talk is not just that we make our reasoning explicit but that alternatives are offered and explored rationally.

A collaboration is the sort of conversation where we actively build on what the other has to say.

The emphasis is not simply on arriving at a shared understanding but on doing so in a mutually supportive manner. By contrast with the exchange, the collaboration is less critical. It is built more on the development of a warm relationship than on the cool foundations of logic. Its foundation is in co-operation. Often the most evident clue to this sort of talk is the speed and enthusiasm with which we adopt the other person's ideas, or allow our own to be adapted and developed.

So what?

Well, it helps to be able to recognize what sort of conversation we're in because that gives us a clue about what's going on, about where the other person is coming from. And it's even more helpful to know what sort of conversation we might be going into because that gives us some choice over how we prepare for it and how we shape it in the moment. Because at one time or another we will find ourselves in each of these types of conversation. It's not that one is always best and one is worst while the third is some mediocre alternative.

There will be many times when the most effective thing we can do is to exchange views. When the issue is large or complex and would benefit from some extended thinking, for instance. When working together like this can enable us to talk our way to a workable answer, since between us we know enough about the problem or the opportunity to be able to reason a way forward.

There will be other times when the most effective thing we can do is to be collaborative. Again the issue or project may be too large or complex for us to resolve by ourselves and we are going to need each other's help and support to see it through to a successful conclusion. A collaborative conversation is perhaps especially important where we can't simply reach a workable solution in a single sitting, situations of greater uncertainty where features and consequences only become apparent over time and we have to go forward together, jointly exploring and building a solution.

talking action

clued up

momentum

There will even be times when the most effective thing we can do is to be confrontational. When we are right and the other person is wrong, for example. Or, since things are seldom so black and white in practice, when we judge that giving in or making a concession is simply too risky. Allowing someone to do something which would put them or others in danger would be an extreme example. But there are more everyday instances where it is appropriate for us to be confrontational, such as when we are faced with someone who is speaking confrontationally and won't respond to our efforts to move the discussion into a more productive exchange or collaboration. In that case we'd better be even better than they are at confrontational conversation or we're going to find ourselves backing down when it isn't appropriate to do so.

Conversational moves

These are the three types of conversation, but as we've said, conversation is dynamic. It's about moves. So what moves can we make? What options are available? Essentially three. A move towards each of the points of the conversational range. We've named the moves to reflect their purpose: the Counter, the Reinforce and the Probe.

Counter, Reinforce, Probe. Strip conversations back to basics (and we know that's what we're doing, for the sake of clarity) and these are the three moves open to us in conversation.

The Counter is an expression of disagreement. It may be defensive, in response to what someone else has said, or it may be more pre-emptive, stating your position. Either way, the move is essentially a blocker. It is designed to force the interaction either towards or away from a particular direction. What does it sound like? *'No.' 'I disagree.' 'I don't accept that.' 'What I need here is this.' 'You're wrong.' 'I'm right and here's why.'*

The Reinforce is an expression of agreement. Again you may use it either as a response, an expression of support, or more proactively, perhaps as an exhortation or a reminder. Either way, as a move it is essentially an accelerator. It is designed to nudge the interaction in a certain direction.

What does it sound like? *'Yes.' 'I agree.' 'Also we could…' 'I think you're absolutely right.' 'What I'd like to add to that is…'*

You'll have noticed that the common factor behind both these moves is that in each case we're reasonably sure about things, about what we want, about where the other person is coming from and so on. Sure. Clued up. And when we are clued up, these are very appropriate moves. But, as we've seen, much of the time we're not as clued up as we need to be effective and get things done. That's why we've drawn the conversational triangle balanced precariously on its tip rather than resting on a solid foundation. Too often our conversations are not based on a solid foundation of clues. That's why the 'don't know' region is such an important part of this particular framework. That's why the Probe move is so important. It builds the foundations without which the Counter and the Reinforce moves can so often produce unintended, and undesirable, effects.

So what is the Probe? It's an expression of inquiry. It's designed to reduce uncertainty, to open things up, explore them, resolve puzzles and establish understanding, in other words create a basis for deciding what directions are viable. A vital move to have in your repertoire. What does it sound like? *'Let's explore that before we decide.' 'Another way of looking at that might be…' 'Let's consider the alternatives.' 'What would be the implications of that?' 'What are the various pros and cons?'*

So conversations can be treated as a series of moves which we make, whether initiating them or in response to what the other parties to the conversation are doing.

An essentially simple range of choices. Handy, in a complex or fast-moving situation, in the moment, when we simply don't have the mental resources to try to remember the fine print of all the personal effectiveness stuff.

Have one more look at the model.

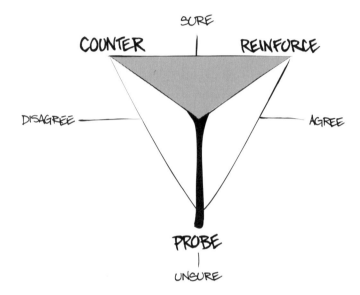

Notice the shape of the range of moves, the range of action. If we feel sure about what's going on, we've got some freedom to manoeuvre. We can agree or disagree, or have some qualified or conditional level of agreement somewhere in between. But when we're unsure about what's going on then we're boxed in. The range of effective behaviours is much narrower. Our only safe route is to move vertically, up the thick line on our model. Getting clued up is the priority. Probing and inquiring are the means of doing that.

Finding the words to carry out the moves

Now here's a little puzzle. If the counter, the reinforce and the probe are the moves, how do we make them? Through words. So what words have we got to carry out these actions? It's worth thinking about, because having verbal range really increases our ability to do things through words.

So here's the challenge. How many words can you think of for expressing each of the three moves? They don't have to be expressions (we're going to encourage you to do that in the final episode). For the moment single words will do. See if you can come up with 20 different words for each move.

	COUNTER	REINFORCE	PROBE
1.			
2.			
3.			
4.			
5.			
6.			
7.			
8.			
9.			
10.			
11.			
12.			
13.			
14.			
15.			
16.			
17.			
18.			
19.			
20.			

There are certainly a lot to choose from. Confession time: when we got stuck, we consulted the thesaurus (another way of getting clued up). Here's our list. We're not suggesting these all have the same meaning. But they are kindred. They are the families of our three moves, harder and softer relatives. As you read through the lists, if you find yourself reacting rather differently to some of these variants just make a mental note of how. (By the way, they're mostly verbs, just to keep the accent on 'doing' words.)

Counter

antagonize	argue	attack	block	boomerang
challenge	clash	collide	confront	contend
counter-attack	deactivate	demur	dissent	hinder
inhibit	intimidate	moderate	object	obstruct
oppose	parry	prevent	protest	punish
push back	quarrel	rebuff	refuse	repel
repulse	resist	restrain	retaliate	revolt
riposte	undo	withstand		

Reinforce

abet	augment	amplify	accelerate	accommodate
affirm	aggrandize	aggravate	animate	appreciate
assist	back	boost	champion	comfort
develop	distend	distort	encourage	endorse
energize	enlarge	exacerbate	exaggerate	excite
expand	extend	favour	help	hot up
increase	inflate	intensify	invigorate	lift
magnify	multiply	nourish	oblige	progress
proliferate	prolong	promote	protract	refresh
relieve	safeguard	snowball	sponsor	spoon-feed
spread	subsidize	stimulate	strengthen	succour
supplement	support			

Probe

assess	cast about	check out	comb
confer	consider	delve	dialogue
discover	discuss	estimate	examine
experiment	explore	fish for	gauge
go over	grill	inquire	inquisition
interrogate	investigate	prospect	pry
query	question	rummage	sample
search	seek	sound out	speculate
test	try out	verify	

What point are we making? Several.

First, we're not saying that all of these are everyday expressions in your occupational life. However, we are suggesting that they might be. The sheer richness of language available to express the three basic conversational moves is a wonderful resource. And one of the reasons our talk so often fails to achieve action is, as we pointed out earlier, that we over-rely on a narrow, impoverished sub-set. Consequently our speech becomes tired, dulled and blunted. It lacks freshness. It fails to alert, enable or inspire.

Second, we'd suggest the fact that the language has so many words related to the three basic conversational moves tells us how much time we must spend making those moves, or variations on them. Because the variations extend our range of action. They allow us to make finer distinctions in our reading of what's going on. But we have to have the words to do this. We mentioned in passing at the beginning of this angle that language can help our thinking because it's the principal currency that we use. So, if we want to be clued up, able to pick up the clues and make good sense of them, it's worth having the language to do it with.

We wrote earlier about the importance of good thinking and of actively managing our thinking. One of the things that enables us to think well is having the language to do it with. Language that is rich and varied gives us the ability to think more openly and with greater depth. It enables us to categorize things, and not become stuck in one particular way of looking at them. Having wordpower enables us to develop alternative ways of framing and making sense of what's going on around us, identifying and articulating alternative choices for action. As someone we worked with once put it, *'It's hard to deal with something if you don't have a name for it.'*

A third point about our word lists is that they illustrate how the three moves can produce unintended and undesirable effects.

How did you react for instance to words like *antagonize* and *punish*, *exaggerate* and *spoon-feed*, *grill* and *inquisition*? Speech is something we need to handle with care. That's why we all tend to speak indirectly. Because we want to secure the other person's agreement without losing their regard or our own freedom of action. Which is simply a form of the openness dilemma that we discussed in the politics angle. So this is another reason why it's worth developing our wordpower. Having more ways of expressing the three basic moves gives us more scope to finesse and control the impact of our speech acts.

Where do we go from here?

There's more to say about coming up with the words that make things happen, but they are best said in context. Your context. That's where we'll see whether we've got this particular idea across the idea-action gap.

The basic message of this angle is a simple one.

Words have power because – or more precisely when – they shape thinking and action, both our own and other people's. Yet we tend to be less mindful in our use of language than we should be. Giving this more attention, both before and during the event, offers a high payback in terms of effective performance.

This can be supported by knowing what territory you are in when you are having conversations. To choose the right moves. Do you know enough about what is going on? Do you agree or not? What type of conversation are you having?

So that's where we're going from here, into a two-part episode. A generic episode. A first part to develop your talking repertoire, and a final part to give you an episode organizer, where you can draw on the various angles that we've covered and apply them to your own situations, ideas and projects.

an episode on
talking action

Good talking is even more demanding than good thinking as you have less control over it. A point we made in the last angle. To help respond in the moment we described a simple organizer to let you know where you are in the conversation. In an exchange and probing, for instance.

Unfortunately you still have to come up with the goods. You can deliver good or bad collaboration. You have to improvise effectively.

How do you improvise?

Ask a jazz musician. We did. And this is what she said.

You listen to the others and go from them, like they pick up on you. You catch the mood and find the notes to match the chords. It's a vibe. Everyone aims to match it. It's like a conversation. You go on from what has already happened and you use the knowledge of the forms. You know their music and other music too. You have a memory bank of other people's improvisations and you play with that. Then you shift the volume and tone to fit the moment.

What a brilliant metaphor for conversation. She even makes the link herself! The secret seems to be twofold. First to be clued up (well, we would say that), to spot the vibe, the mood, the chords. And second to have a large repertoire of improvisations to draw on (and to choose the right ones, of course).

This episode is aimed at the latter, building your conversational repertoire.

Avoid limiting your repertoire

There are a number of comparatively simple, and certainly very learnable, techniques that are extremely useful for enabling our talk to have the effects that we desire. Techniques that will give us that important repertoire to choose from. But before we look at a few of these, let's just register how clumsy and poorly developed our 'talking action' can be.

Here are a couple of things to listen for, symptoms of a shortfall in the action talking department.

First, the buzzword. Start listening for it as soon as you get to work. We bet there'll be one along in a minute. What will it be? *Teamwork*, perhaps, or *continuous improvement*, or *process re-engineering*, or *learning organization*. The real problem is not with these concepts but with the way they're used in speech. It's not that these phrases are wrong but that they're shallow. They are used as substitutes for explanation. So they make for default thinking and discussions that don't resolve issues. Part of their deception is the glittery allure of the fashionable. They're so widely used, so current. How uncool not to know what these things mean, or to have to ask. We have had people come to us for coaching saying they 'want some of that management speak'. Needless to say, what they get instead is encouragement to challenge every buzzword and cliché they ever encounter. *'So what exactly do you mean?'* is such a powerful question.

Language has a hierarchical structure. Words, or the concepts that they represent, are sub-sets of each other, as shown in the following diagram.

The same words will appear in different concept hierarchies and the nature of any hierarchy is quite personal. Our picture of personal growth may be very different from yours.

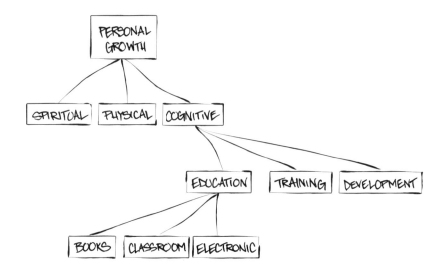

Buzzwords are an example of a poor use of high-level or large concept words. They mask the meaning. Questions like *'So what exactly do you mean?'* or *'How specifically…'* or *'What precisely…'* all have the effect of moving down the hierarchy. What NLP (Neuro-Linguistic Programming) calls 'chunking down'.

Often conversations stall because we are each talking at different levels in the hierarchy.

It is often best to start at a level where you can gain agreement. This may mean 'chunking up' by asking questions such as, *'For what purpose?'* or *'Why?'*. At a higher level it is easier to reach agreement. For instance, have you ever worked in a company where communication wasn't an issue? A high-concept or big-chunk word like communication is difficult to disagree with. From that agreement you can move to small-chunk concepts where you can start to be clear about where your real differences of opinion lie.

A second clue for identifying ineffective language is the exhausted superlative (our name for it). As the speaker tries harder and harder to make an impact, the words, and especially the adjectives, steadily escalate in a frantic bid to become more convincing. *'Sian's a good candidate for this role…Sian really is a very capable person…Sian's extremely good at this…I have to tell you that in all my years as a manager Sian is the most exceptional…'* Listen for this one. Exaggeration has a steadily diminishing return. It's a great pointer for when language isn't working.

Shaping talk

So what can we do about it? What can we do so that our talk does what we want it to do? What does good sound like?

If you really want to get into it, there's a whole field of study called socio-linguistics, which is revealing what makes talk more or less persuasive. Get on the net and follow that keyword. But here are some clues for starters.

The three-part list

We come across as more persuasive if we support what we have to say with evidence. That's as it should be and it's good thinking practice to consider both sides of the argument in depth, to search for and uncover several pros and several cons. But when it comes to speaking, you can overdo it. When you're advocating an argument, it seems (from analysis of successful public speakers) that a three-part list of reasons is the most persuasive. Two is too few. Four is too many. The three-part list seems to have a form of beginning, middle and end structure that not only sounds comprehensive and manageable for the listener but also signals its own completion. *'So I recommend Sian as a candidate. She has several years of relevant experience, she is technically accomplished, and she has the perseverance to stick with this difficult role.'*

Contrasts

An even simpler linguistic device is the contrast. *'Ella has the youth and the enthusiasm, but Toni has the experience and the know-how.'* Once again there is something about the shape of the utterance, in this case its symmetry, that seems to make it sound more balanced, more equitable and more compelling when you're listening.

Headline-punchline

This is a particular form of contrast, you might call it 'the dramatic comparison'. *'We were wrong when we said the new procedures would save 20 per cent in 12 months…they saved 30 per cent in six months.'*

Puzzle-solution

A variation of headline-punchline is to pose the first part of the statement as a question. Not only does this engage the listener's attention and curiosity but it also heralds the arrival of the answer. A way of giving it greater emphasis. *'What enabled us to come to an agreement?…Being prepared to find out each other's concerns.'*

These are rhetorical devices. You might regard them as tricks of the speaker's trade, but you disregard them at your peril. Research shows that they work. So, even if you are reluctant to use them yourself, you had better be alert to them and their impact when other people are using them.

Because, as we've said already, talking action is not a solitary pursuit. It's all about interaction. So much of what we set out to achieve in our working lives is stuff that we cannot get done by ourselves. We need others to do things to help us (or not do things that will hinder). That's why so much of our talking is about negotiating what things mean, why they matter and what is to be done.

Shaping conversations

This makes all important conversations potentially a contest of interests. Which takes us back to politics and the dilemma of being open about our intentions. If we are open, people are likely to trust us but may try to take advantage of our openness. If we're more closed, there may be less risk of being manipulated, but there is more risk of being distrusted. (Note the use of contrast for persuasive effect in that last sentence.)

So how do we tend to deal with this dilemma when we're conversing?

By being indirect.

The bind is that we want to get other people's acceptance and agreement without abandoning our own freedom of action.

The problem with saying exactly what we mean is that this puts both at risk. Consequently, as language expert Deborah Tannen points out, we seek to be understood without saying explicitly what we mean. Because this approach offers two big payoffs. First, a greater prospect of establishing and maintaining rapport with the other person. Second, better self-defence.

How exactly do we do this?

Once again there are a number of common devices.

Many of them are to do with establishing our credibility. Here are three.

At first…but then

Like all these devices, this one is a means of advocating a position while simultaneously leaving ourselves some room to manoeuvre. *'At first I thought that what she said made sense, but then after a while I wasn't so sure.'* It gives the impression of having invested consideration. An impression. In itself it doesn't provide much evidence of good thinking.

Reported speech

Another way of creating a sense of objectivity is by using reported speech. *'It's said that establishing the service support centre in Edinburgh will release people to take on new business development roles here in London.'* As the speaker you can voice an opinion while retaining the freedom to associate yourself with or distance yourself from it, depending on your listener's reaction.

Passive tense

Using a passive rather than an active tense has a similar effect. It leaves some vagueness about responsibility. *'The IT people and the project team are going to be co-located.'*

In themselves these may all seem like small things, hardly worth bothering about. But compare the impact of the examples given above with the following comparisons.

◆ *'I think she's talking nonsense.'*

◆ *'Establishing the service support centre in Edinburgh will release people to take on new business development roles here in London.'*

◆ *'I've decided that the IT people and the project team are to be co-located.'*

Now imagine that the listener disagrees with the speaker. Where's that conversation going? And who's in control of it?

That should be enough by way of examples to alert you to listen out for linguistic tricks. We're on the verge of falling into that familiar trap of creating too much to remember. So let's recognize that pitfall and keep moving.

Listening

A final word on listening. We have been focusing on hints and tips for building your repertoire of options. To help you be effective in probing, countering or reinforcing. To make the right choices you have to listen to the rest of the conversation. Remember the jazz musician, picking up on the mood and vibe, listening for the chords to choose her notes. You have to listen to what others say. It is rich in clues.

As you listen to conversations you will be able to spot patterns. They are clues to where someone is coming from, how they really think or feel. The world of NLP has developed many techniques in this area, building particularly on the work of American hypno-therapist Milton Erickson. Three important patterns to look out for in others' language (and your own for that matter) are as follows.

Distortions

This is where the choice of words implies a particular situation that is not necessarily true. A common example is where we talk as if we can read the minds of others. *'You don't want me to do this.'* *'You think I am too young.'* We can never know what others are thinking, only they know (sometimes!). Another common distortion is to make a judgement about something, but to lose sight of the person who is doing the judging. For instance, *'It is wrong to jump to conclusions', 'You have to love someone totally before you can marry them'.*

Generalizations

We develop encompassing patterns that miss out important information. Words like *never, every, everyone* hide counter examples of what we are talking about, as in the classic *'Nobody loves me'* or *'I'll never do that again'.* Likewise, sentences which start with *'I mustn't…, ought not to…, have to…'* are clues to missing causes and effects.

Deletions

Also look out for missing or deleted information. Phrases like *'I am happy'* (about what?) or sentences where responsibility is unclear. *'They are all out to get me.'* Another example is the incomplete comparison, deleting the person or thing to which the comparison is made. *'She was worse.'* Or combining this with a generalization, *'It was the best party ever'.*

When these phrases are used they often provide clues about where someone is coming from. What this person has presupposed in order to make that statement. This is all about reading between the lines.

Conversationally an appropriate response to these patterns is to ask questions which seek to replace or uncover the missing or hidden information. These can often be challenging, but delivered in an inquiring way can unearth much more information. This prompts a more direct conversation and helps to avoid the ambiguities described above. So, for instance, *'You think I am too young'* could prompt the response, *'What makes you think that?'.*

'I'll never do that again' could lead to *'Never?'* or perhaps *'What would happen if you did do that again?'*

'Who, exactly, is out to get you?' might be a response to *'They are all out to get me'.*

Probe to understand distortions, generalizations and deletions.

So where does all this leave me?

Much of your action in the gap will be through the words you use. At the same time other people's choice of words and structuring of sentences give many clues to where they are coming from. In this episode we have attempted to raise your awareness of some of the things to do and to look for. Our main hope is that this will give you enough of a start to continue to observe what goes on around you. This observation, reflection (good thinking) on what you see and testing out new approaches will be the way for you to build your repertoire of conversational responses. We want you to operate in the gap as naturally as a jazz saxophonist on a steamy Saturday night in New Orleans!

So let's give the last word to another jazz musician. (Yes, we asked two.) He's from Boston. His thoughts not only sum up this episode beautifully but touch on many of the ideas we've presented about being clued up.

…improvisation…it's wonderfully frightening… live without a net is a scary thing. Trust is key. What's the process? Well, in my experience usually someone has an idea and just plunges ahead. Others borrow from that idea or complement it in some way from their own ideas. It's a lot about listening for feel…is this building up, down, remaining the same, is it erratic, stationary, what's the energy in the story? In a way it's like figuring out the emotional content in the story.

Typically there's a lot of interaction outside of the music, too – eye contact, a gesture, a grimace, a nod. These are important, particularly when the players don't really know each other well…

What are the clues and cues?

It's interesting that in jazz there are many pre-established rules, formats, and changes that many will use when improvising. Like improv comedy – if you don't know these hidden forms it's downright impossible to leap in and improv with a bunch of players. I can't tell you how many people I've played with only once simply because they pissed off others in how they stepped all over the creative process. So being facile with these forms is key.

How do you choose a response?

Typically in playing drums there's a level of activity that is pretty unconscious – you can chug out a rhythm without really thinking about it. So your mind is left to guide on a more general level – I'm not thinking about every touch, every note I'm hitting. I'm thinking more about the feel, the emotion, the centre of the musical story. To respond to what another person has laid out, I guess I think of three options: zig, zag or silence. A zig is to go with the idea, using the same rhythm perhaps altered just a bit. The idea is to create coherence with it. Zag is to purposefully cut against the idea, disrupt it a bit, hit against the rhythm. The idea is to create tension that someone can use to resolve (or build further). Or silence. Just let the idea hang as is and keep chugging underneath it. Choosing which one is very situational – it depends on what has happened before, where the song has come, and where it might go from here.

What makes it easier?

Trusting the others, levels of patience, giving room to each other, knowing where each other is coming from. Knowing your 'voice' – how your instrument speaks with others, its range of tone and dynamics, knowing how it can add, or subtract.

a final glance at Networker

What does the Networker story tell us?

Quite a lot, we would suggest, about the challenge of turning any idea into action. People enlist to support an idea for different reasons, reasons that are unlikely to be fully thought through at the start. They act with the best of intentions. From moment to moment they do what makes sense to them from their particular perspective. But these reasons and perspectives differ and that's where the frictions and collisions start, although they're often muted, because we don't often set out to fall out. So we leave things unsaid, or only partially expressed, although they may be acutely felt. Which means we have to rely more and more on clues. And fall so easily into the twin traps of either misinterpreting or over-interpreting these clues.

And so our views of what's happening, of each other, and of what actions need to be taken, diverge. Often past the point of no return.

Its use here has been to give you a glimpse of the gap, and the clues in it.

This is a rare opportunity. At any other time it can only be done in the moment. We thank all those involved.

And at the time of writing…

The Genesis Association has gone its own way to meet its particular needs.

Kim and Carl, meanwhile, refocused their efforts, developing a set of core modules that could easily be combined to create the collaboration environment they had promised so many months before. They formulated a revised business model that would allow the Genesis Centre to lease Networker for a moderate monthly fee.

They are still working actively with the Genesis Centre to bring the Networker idea into action. The dialogue has its share of exchanges, collaborations and confrontations, but they're still talking. The idea is moving forward. They've kept it moving.

Carl and Kim have just signed an agreement with the Genesis Centre to develop Networker.

talking

clued up

momentum

the episode that goes on

how to get your ideas into action

Depending on how you have chosen to read this book, you may be coming to this particular episode last, first, or somewhere in the middle. In a real sense, it doesn't matter, since this chapter is designed to stand alone. It's about the episode that goes on after you put the book down and get on with whatever it was that prompted you to pick it up in the first place.

The purpose of this chapter is to integrate the various angles that we have covered and to provide you with a way of holding them in your mind when you encounter challenges to your personal effectiveness. It is not organized around our angles (although it shows how we think they relate to each other) but around your ongoing experience.

Whether your immediate concern is with a particular task, or a project, a role, your personal development or your career as a whole, you are in the process of trying to put ideas into action. In the immortal words of Spike Milligan, *'Everybody's got to be somewhere.'* And in our occupational and organizational lives, that somewhere, for most of us, most of the time, is trying to put ideas, of one sort or another, of one size or another, into action. And encountering the difficulties of doing so, the problems of realizing our intentions in practice, the challenge of being effective.

So, what's our story?

It starts with the proposition that ideas often don't make it into action. There's a gap between the thought and the deed, between the intention and the outcome. All too often, performance stumbles and falls in that gap.

Now of course we all know that. That's why people read, and write, books about personal effectiveness. And the basic expectation is that if we absorb the advice that these provide and acquire the requisite skills and techniques, these will bridge the idea-action gap.

The problem is that there is no reliable bridge. There's no easy way over or round the idea-action gap, no techniques that can keep you out of it. You have to work your way *through* the gap because it *is* the situation in which you're working. That's where we live and work. Like it or not, that's where you are, in the idea-action gap.

And when we look at the idea-action gap, what do we find? We find the nub of the challenge.

Often it isn't easy to see what's going on. That's one of the main reasons why being personally effective is so difficult. We need to tailor our actions to the circumstances, but making sense of those circumstances isn't straightforward. Nor is deciding what to do.

So in practice, when we're trying to put an idea into action, we actually find ourselves involved in three ongoing activities:

1 Understanding the context.

2 Generating choices for action.

3 Anticipating the consequences.

These are the activities that we need to be pursuing between the idea and its implementation in order to turn an idea effectively into a reality.

We've numbered these three activities, not to suggest that they are a three-step strategy to success. They're not like that. You can't 'do' number 1, understand the context, then simply leave it behind when you move on to 2, generate your choices, and so on. The process is less structured and more iterative than that. You need to keep at these things. It isn't a guarantee of success, but rather a way of improving the odds of a successful outcome in your favour.

We've numbered these three activities to make the point that, as a set, they are small, manageable and memorable. (Ease of recollection when you need it – that's why there are 3Cs.) Three things to remember to be doing when you're trying – and finding it difficult – to put an important idea into practice. We've made understanding the context number 1 to underline its priority, since choices and consequences can depend so much on the specifics of the context.

So let's expand our picture of the idea-action gap and this time put the emphasis on what we can be doing about it.

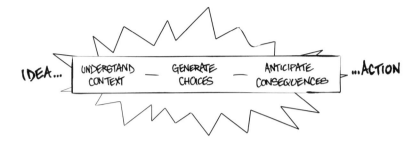

IDEA... UNDERSTAND CONTEXT — GENERATE CHOICES — ANTICIPATE CONSEQUENCES ...ACTION

Put a lot of effort into understanding, and continuing to understand, your context, because it doesn't stand still.

But how can you do that?

By keeping your eyes and ears open. The mouth can be useful too, but should be used more sparingly. Again, there are no sure-fire ways of understanding your context, no three-step solutions to perfect comprehension. Life's too untidy for that. But we can improve the odds. Because there are three sorts of things that you can expect to find – and should expect to find – within the idea-action gap. It's another set of three (except that they don't all start with the letter C this time – told you life was messy!):

1 Clues.

2 Complexity.

3 Politics.

Clues

Expect clues, because life doesn't come spelled out. Complex situations and political behaviours are just the extreme end of a general tendency, which is that behaviour needs to be interpreted. There's nothing sinister in this. That's just the way it is: fast, lots going on, different people pursuing different objectives, or similar objectives with different priorities, lots of talk, lots of thought, not always in the open and even when it is, not always easy to follow.

Open to interpretation, open to misinterpretation. 'Hints and allegations.' Clues are the raw material for our task of understanding context, generating choices and anticipating consequences. Clues are scattered throughout the book. Well they would be, wouldn't they? Like life.

Complexity

Expect complexity, because context – we call it the idea-action gap – *is* messy. That's its nature. It's complex and dynamic, but it's not, contrary to many popular business book titles, truly chaotic. It's not unmanageable. There are patterns in complexity and understanding those patterns informs our choices and our anticipation of consequences. Again, the patterns may not be easy to see until we have some idea about what we might be looking for, and until we actually start to look for them.

Politics

Expect politics, because organizations *are* inevitably political. We may not like that, it may make us feel uncomfortable, but that's their nature. As the number of people in an organization increases, so does the potential for their views and interests to differ, or to be perceived to differ. Hey presto! Political behaviours. Some of these can be easy to see. But some are not. Again, there are informative patterns to be found, if we're prepared to look.

So that's what you should expect to find – and look for – in the idea-action gap, in the time, space and activity between coming up with your idea and getting it into action.

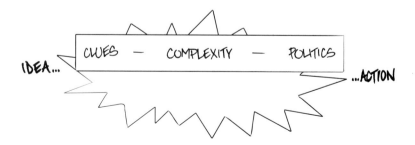

So you've got some sense about what you should expect to encounter, what you should be looking for, and what you should be doing. What else can we take with us on our trek through the gap to improve the chances of getting our ideas, projects and ambitions successfully into action?

It's one more set of three:

1   Minding the gap.

2   Good thinking.

3   Talking action.

What are these? Travelling companions. Ideally, habits that we should cultivate and take with us whenever we're engaged in an endeavour that's important to us or that's likely to be challenging. Habits that will make it easier for us to understand context, generate choices and anticipate consequences.

Minding the gap

We've said a lot about this already. Why is it so important? Because we forget. The actual task of turning ideas into action, of working with others, of picking our way through complexity and politics, of trying to anticipate consequences and create viable choices for action, all this fills up our attention. All these immediate and urgent tasks crowd out the more fundamental and important job of staying alert. Are you paying attention?

Good thinking

This is a book about action. That's what you wanted, wasn't it? Content that would tell you what you can do. Action. Well, paradoxical as it might seem, one of the most useful forms of action is thinking. Good thinking. The trouble is that often our thinking isn't very good. It isn't up to the challenges presented by complex situations, political behaviours and half-glimpsed clues. It isn't up to the challenges presented by having to make sense of our context, generate choices and anticipate consequences. But we can make it better. You can develop your thinking.

Talking action

And here's another paradox. Words are often the most powerful form of action. Because the gap is inhabited. That's the nature of the territory we have to work our way through. Sometimes these people go along with us. Sometimes they get in our way, just as we get in theirs, whether any of us means to or not. Most of the time they're busy pursuing their own paths, whether they're heading towards the same objectives as us, or different ones. How we talk to each other has a lot to do with how well we get through the gap. Unfortunately, this often doesn't get much attention either.

Remember minding the gap.

Remember good thinking.

Remember talking action.

Three things not to leave behind.

There's a standing joke that consultants reduce everything to a 2x2 matrix. Absurd. Too simplistic.

It's 3x3, of course.

Three things to be doing:

1 Understanding the context.

2 Generating choices for action.

3 Anticipating the consequences.

Three things to watch for:

1 Clues.

2 Complexity.

3 Politics.

Three things to take with you:

1 Minding the gap.

2 Good thinking.

3 Talking action.

There's a great joke at the end of Douglas Adams's book *The Hitch-Hiker's Guide to the Galaxy* (Pan, 1988), where the hero finally discovers the answer, to life, the universe and everything. The answer is 42.

So what are we saying? That these nine things are the 'answer'? That these nine things are personal effectiveness?

No. Personal effectiveness is not a commodity. Being personally effective is a pursuit, an ongoing challenge, and paying attention is at the heart of it.

There is no answer.

The truth is not out there.

But there are some great questions. Questions to facilitate the tasks of understanding your context, generating choices and anticipating consequences. Questions to enable you to get clued up and find your own answers to the challenges that stand between you and turning your ideas into action.

In the moment, you may not have an answer, but you likely have the questions. So we'd encourage you to put more energy into devising and pursuing your own questions rather than waiting for other people's answers. Because questions are the fuel for being, and staying, clued up, in context.

But a final word of caution. Questions by themselves are not much use either. You have to do something with them. Put the answers to work. Let's illustrate with an example from the research for this book. Our interviewee was describing how he'd spotted a clue, noticed an abrupt change in the mood of a meeting in which he'd been involved.

I thought, whoa! What on earth's going on here?

What did you do with that thought? we asked.

Ah…(pauses). Now, you come to mention it, nothing.

States the problem rather neatly, really.

So we're handing this episode over to you, because it has to be yours.

Only you can do something with it now.

In handing over, what are we giving you?

We're offering you a map of the territory. Like most maps, some of its features are familiar, others are less so. To get the most from it, to become a seasoned traveller, you need to visit the places marked on it and spend some time in each of them. Unlike most maps, however, this is one for many journeys because it depicts the territory we have to go through time and time again during our occupational and organizational lives.

Here's the map. We've made it handily small.

THINGS TO BE UNDERSTOOD (THE LESS OBVIOUS STUFF)	CLUES — COMPLEXITY — POLITICS
THINGS TO BE DOING (THE MORE OBVIOUS STUFF)	UNDERSTAND THE CONTEXT GENERATE CHOICES ANTICIPATE CONSEQUENCES
THINGS TO REMEMBER (THE STUFF THAT TENDS TO GET FORGOTTEN)	MINDING THE GAP — GOOD THINKING — TALKING ACTION

How does this map work? Consult it before you embark on your project, whatever that project is. Or use it when you're lost. It works then too, because even if it doesn't tell you where you are, it will prompt you, either on where you're trying to go, or what to look for, or how to go about getting there most effectively.

What's the route through your particular territory? It's your territory, your context, your idea-action gap, so it needs to be your route. But here's a clue (naturally). Don't expect the route to be direct. Don't expect to travel smoothly from left to right across this map. Expect to move around it. Expect to visit some squares, maybe most squares, more than once in the course of any journey. Be prepared to go back in order to go forward. It's a process of making sense and moving on, making sense and moving on, making sense and moving on…

Try the map now.

Here's the START…

What's your idea? What are you trying to achieve?

Is it a project that you're trying to implement, a design that you're trying to complete, an opinion you're trying to shift, a job that you're trying to get, a career change that you're trying to effect? What's your idea?

Write in the book, if you want. That's okay, if you've bought it.

Where are you now? What's your context? Are you minding the gap?

Here are some questions to get you started.

◆ What's going on here?

◆ Who is involved? In what ways?

◆ What are their particular interests and concerns?

◆ How does this situation behave?

◆ Why does it work like that?

◆ What are the various things contributing to this situation?

◆ What are the unobvious contributors?

What are you intending to do next? What are your choices?

How good is your thinking?

Here are some more questions to help you.

- What could you do here? What options are there?

- What other alternatives can you think up?

- What constraints are there?

- How real are those constraints?

- What are the less obvious courses of action?

- Who do you need to speak to?

- What sort of conversation do you need that to be?

- How are you going to frame that?

What's likely to happen? What consequences can you expect?

Have you done justice to the complexity that you're working with? How's it likely to unfold over time? Have you made sense of the politics?

Some more questions:

◆ What effects (plural) might that action be expected to produce?

◆ Where might that lead?

◆ In what ways might that change how things work at the moment?

◆ What problems – and opportunities – might that create?

◆ How are people most likely to react to that?

◆ What further repercussions might that have?

◆ Which are most probable?

◆ What unobvious consequences might be foreseen?

Not even sure where you are on the map?

Time to make a broader sweep. Look for some clues. There's sure to be some around.

Here are some questions to help you find them.

◆ What have you noticed recently?

◆ What has surprised or puzzled you recently?

◆ What might that mean?

◆ How else could you look at this?

◆ What other angle could you take on this?

◆ What might this be saying about the context you're working in?

◆ What might this be saying about your choices for action?

◆ What might this be saying about the consequences of your choices?

It's your moment. It's your move.

What are you going to pay attention to now?

appendix

How do you handle conflict?

There are a number of distinct approaches to handling disagreements. Research and organizational consultants Ken Thomas and Ralph Kilmann developed a simple model summarizing these approaches. We have created a short questionnaire to help you identify your preferred approaches within this model. Understanding your own style is the first step in being a good handler of conflict.

Throughout this book, we've placed a heavy emphasis on the importance of the situation and its influence on your behaviour.

Therefore our questionnaire is structured around a series of, probably, familiar situations. Analyzing your answers will give you an opportunity not only to consider the overall pattern of results but the impact of the type of situation as well.

Imagine yourself in each of the following situations and then decide how you would be most likely to respond. There are five choices in each case. Identify your most likely choice as number 1, and mark your next most likely response as number 2. Then go on to the next situation.

For this exercise to be most informative, you need to try to imagine how you have actually behaved in similar situations in the past.

1 **You have put a lot of work into preparing a written proposal for your manager, who has returned it with little apparent consideration, only a scribbled note at the foot of the final page saying, 'Give this more thought.'**
   a. I would put the proposal to one side and do something else.
   b. I would make an appointment to discuss the matter.
   c. I would modify the bits I didn't feel particularly strongly about.
   d. I'd find out what my manager wanted. **1**
   e. I'd go and explain why I believed the proposal was right. **2**

2 **You are expecting an important telephone call and have asked not to be disturbed on any account, when a colleague taps you on the shoulder wanting to discuss your late input to her urgent report.**
   a. I would attend to the report and delay taking the call.
   b. I would state firmly that I had asked not to be disturbed.
   c. I would ask her to leave the report so I could do it while waiting for the call and complete it directly afterwards. **2**
   d. I would apologize and ask her when I needed to give her the input. **1**
   e. I would explain the importance of the call and try to find a time when I could provide the input she needed.

3 In a meeting of your peer group, you have just explained why you don't agree with an idea put forward by one of your colleagues. With a raised voice the colleague suggests that you simply don't know what you're talking about.

   a. I'd tell them why I thought they were wrong.

   b. I'd say I hadn't meant to offend them.

   c. I'd try to clarify why we both felt the way we did. 1

   d. I wouldn't push the point. 2

   e. I'd see if someone else could reconcile our views.

4 You have just received what you consider to be an unjust piece of feedback from your manager during your performance evaluation discussion.

   a. I'd argue the point.

   b. I'd probably say I didn't accept that, but I might not say much more. 2

   c. I'd say I thought it was unfair and suggest a modification of the point.

   d. I'd ask what they wanted me to do.

   e. I'd try to understand why they felt that way. 1

5 A colleague makes a sweeping criticism of your department, suggesting that this is typical of its performance.

   a. I'd try to get them to take a more balanced view.

   b. I'd ask them to explain the particular problem. 1

   c. I'd defend my department vigorously.

   d. I'd say I was sorry to hear it and ask for their feedback. 2

   e. I wouldn't waste my time on the conversation.

6 A client makes a specific criticism of your department's performance.

   a. I'd offer to make it up to them in some way.

   b. I'd try to get mitigating factors taken into account.

   c. I'd try to schedule to discuss it once they had cooled off a bit.

   d. I'd explain why it had happened. 1

   e. I'd see if we could work out how to prevent the problem recurring. 2

7 You are scheduled to attend an off-site seminar which has been booked for a long time and which you consider important for your continuing professional development. The day before the seminar you get a phone call from your boss's secretary relaying, but not explaining, the message that you need to be in the office tomorrow.

   a. I would contact my boss to find out why I needed to be in the office. *1*

   b. I would cancel the seminar.

   c. I would explain to my boss that I was on a seminar. *2*

   d. I'd attempt to find a way to do my boss's work during the seminar.

   e. I'd phone in sick in the morning and go to the seminar anyway.

8 You have just returned to work having spent the previous day at an off-site seminar that you considered important for your continuing professional development. Your manager summons you and tells you that this is not how you are expected to spend your time and that you are not to do it again.

   a. I'd stand up for my decision to attend the seminar. *2*

   b. I'd either apologize or say that it wouldn't happen again.

   c. I'd agree with him in principle but ask him to see this as a special case.

   d. I'd keep quiet and get the telling-off over with as quickly as possible.

   e. I'd seek to establish some principles for making such decisions. *1*

9 A member of your team is persistently late for work but has a particular technical skill on which you are dependent. This morning the individual arrives one hour late and simply shrugs his shoulders and grins when you point this out.

   a. I'd shrug my shoulders too and walk away.

   b. I'd appeal to their sense of responsibility to other members of the team. *2*

   c. I'd say I'd overlook it on this occasion, if it didn't happen again.

   d. I'd persist until we both understood the problem and had resolved it. *P*

   e. I'd summon him into a disciplinary interview.

10 Having a quick cup of coffee before going to a meeting, you ask your assistant to bring you some papers, only to receive the snappy reply, 'What do you think I am, a mind-reader!'

   a. I'd offer to make them a coffee too while they fetched the papers.

   b. I'd try to find out what was troubling them. *2*

   c. I'd tell them, 'Mind reader or not, just fetch the papers.'

   d. I'd apologize for being insensitive.

   e. I'd keep my head down till the storm had blown over. *1*

11 Staff turnover is increasing in your department. Your manager tells you that this reflects on you and that you need to improve your leadership.

   a. I'd promise to get on to it straight away.

   b. I'd explain why staff turnover was increasing and ask for some advice.

   c. I'd ask for her tips on leadership. *2*

   d. I'd ask her to take the particular circumstances into consideration.

   e. I'd tell her what I was already doing about it. *1*

12 An important client calls you and says that in view of the relationship between your businesses, he hopes that you can provide holiday employment for a teenage relative who is – he adds – with him at that moment.

   a. I'd say I'd be delighted to arrange something. *2*

   b. I'd make it clear that I was looking for something in return.

   c. I'd point out that this gave me an ethical problem.

   d. I'd explain that I'd get human resources to give her a call.

   e. I'd arrange to find out whether this would be possible or problematic. *1*

13 During a performance evaluation discussion an experienced member of your team says that it's your fault that she has not fully met her objectives, since you have not provided clear priorities. You have been holding one-to-one meetings with this person, but they have been relatively infrequent.

   a. I'd concentrate on understanding the issues that we needed to work on.   1

   b. I'd make it clear that the prime responsibility for results is hers.

   c. I'd concentrate on re-establishing our working relationship.

   d. I'd stress the need to look forwards rather than backwards.

   e. I'd suggest that we were both partially responsible for what had happened.   2

14 During a performance evaluation discussion an inexperienced member of your team complains angrily that it's your fault that he has not fully met his objectives, since you have not provided clear priorities. You have, however, been having regular meetings with this person since they started.

   a. I'd accept that I hadn't done enough to help him.

   b. I'd suggest that we were both partially responsible for what had happened.

   c. I'd postpone the meeting until he'd calmed down.

   d. I'd concentrate on creating a jointly agreed agenda for the meeting.   2

   e. I'd remind him that the prime responsibility for results is his.   1

15 You are introducing some changes in your department and have been holding extensive two-way communications to ensure that your people feel informed and involved. This morning you have received a deputation complaining that there is not enough communication about the changes.

   a. I'd explain that we all had to work at making the communications successful.

   b. I'd arrange to see them at another time.

   c. I'd try to understand what had prompted this visit to happen now.   1

   d. I'd remind them how much time I'd already given to communication.   2

   e. I'd try to tell them what they wanted to know.

Now insert three conflict situations drawn directly from your own experience, and again select the choices which most closely reflect your primary and secondary responses.

16 A conflict with a subordinate:

Doug Allen — e d.
John Longdon — e b.

a. I pursued my own needs strongly.
b. I proposed a middle ground.
c. I tried not to get involved.
d. I tried to repair the relationship.
e. I tried to get both sets of concerns into the open.

17 A conflict with a peer or a client:

Bill Thomson   Orion CNr
— b   e.

a. I pursued my own needs strongly.
b. I proposed a middle ground.
c. I tried not to get involved.
d. I tried to repair the relationship.
e. I tried to get both sets of concerns into the open.

18 A conflict of opinion with your manager:

IDS orion Coth.   — a   e.

a. I pursued my own needs strongly.
b. I proposed a middle ground.
c. I tried not to get involved.
d. I tried to repair the relationship.
e. I tried to get both sets of concerns into the open.

There are various ways of examining the patterns in your responses.

But before you get into the analysis, let's make sure you go about it in a clued up way.

What is this analysis going to give you?

Clues. Not answers, not certainties, but pointers. Indications of how you tend to go about it when you find yourself in a particular type of situation.

There are no right answers. The five styles of handling conflict are choices and each choice has its own consequences. Some of these consequences will be more desirable than others, but that will depend on the context.

It's a matter of judgement. Making a clued up choice.

The other reason for offering you this questionnaire is therefore to give you a clearer idea of what the choices look like. To stimulate you to recall conflict situations from your own experience. Which should help you to keep in mind the sorts of consequences that flow from each of the choices.

So there is no set way of analysing your responses.

Here are some possibilities.

Firstly, you can get a picture of whether you tend to rely on certain conflict-handling styles rather than others. Using the grid below, circle the letter that was your first choice in each situation. Then add up the number of times you used that style. It is likely that one or two of the five styles will emerge as the ones you use most often. The absolute numbers are less important than the ranking.

Style preferences:

	Force	Resolve	Compromise	Avoid	Concede
1	(e)	b	c	a	(d)
2	(b)	e	(c)	(d)	a
3	a	(c)	e	(d)	b
4	a	(e)	c	(b)	d
5	c	(b)	a	e	(e)
6	(d)	(e)	b	c	a
7	(c)	(a)	d	e	b
8	(a)	(e)	c	d	b
9	e	(d)	c	a	(b)
10	c	(b)	a	(e)	d
11	(e)	b	d	a	(c)
12	c	(e)	b	d	(a)
13	b	(a)	(e)	d	c
14	(e)	(d)	b	c	a
15	(d)	(c)	a	b	e
16	a	(e)	b	c	(d)
17	a	(e)	(b)	c	d
18	(a)	(e)	b	c	d
TOTALS:	8	15	3	4	6

Now you have an idea about the styles that you generally prefer to use. But what does that mean? What is the essence of each of these styles?

Forcing is a competitive, challenging style, which puts the accent on getting what *you* want. It can serve to push the pace and to make things happen, but it runs the risk of leaving others feeling ignored or overwhelmed and can damage relationships.

Resolving is a collaborative, problem-solving style, which seeks a thorough understanding of both parties' issues so that their respective needs can be met as fully as possible. It's a robust approach, but takes time and can feel blunt.

Compromising is a judicious style, which emphasises give and take. It's a flexible approach, which can be useful, especially if a compromise is the best you're going to get, but, by definition, it is likely to feel less than fully satisfactory and may only produce temporary solutions.

Avoiding can be a tactful and diplomatic style which serves to prevent the disagreement from escalating. It can be useful for controlling the timing of when to confront an issue, but there is a danger of being seen as evasive and uncommitted.

Conceding is an accommodating style which puts the other person's needs first. In effect it gives priority to maintaining rather than risking the relationship. Using it, you may be seen as supportive and helpful, but also perhaps as easily dominated.

Do you show a preference for particular styles? What are the consequences of those preferences?

A second way of analysing your responses is to see whether they vary by type of situation. You can use the grids below for this purpose. The situations in our questionnaire differ primarily in terms of the type of relationship involved. Sometimes this is your manager, at other times a colleague or a member of staff, or a client. Inevitably political and power differences mean that your position will vary from one type of relationship to another. You are likely to find that your approach to handling the potential conflict differs accordingly. Whether it differs appropriately is another question, and we look at that in more depth in our angle on talking action.

Situational analysis:

Relationships with your manager

	Force	Resolve	Compromise	Avoid	Concede
1	e	b	c	a	d
4	a	e	c	b	d
7	c	a	d	e	b
8	a	e	c	d	b
11	e	b	d	a	c
18	a	e	b	c	d

Relationships with your staff

	Force	Resolve	Compromise	Avoid	Concede
9	e	d	c	a	b
10	c	b	a	e	d
13	b	a	e	d	c
14	e	d	b	c	a
15	d	c	a	b	e
16	a	e	b	c	d

Relationships with peers and client

	Force	Resolve	Compromise	Avoid	Concede
2	b	e	c	d	a
3	a	c	e	d	b
5	c	b	a	e	d
6	d	e	b	c	a
12	c	e	b	d	a
17	a	e	b	c	d

Can you see any pattern in your responses?

What might be the consequences of the choices you tend to make?

A third piece of analysis is to examine how you shift from one style to another. Often we try to deal with conflict situations using our preferred style and then, if that doesn't work, move to our next preference. The conflict-handling styles map opposite shows how the different styles relate to each other in terms of assertiveness and co-operation. By looking at how you (and others) move from one style to another, you can get deeper insight into what's going on and clues about what might be needed to make the interaction more effective.

From the questionnaire, take one particular situation that felt particularly resonant for you and note your first and second style choices. Draw this movement onto the conflict-handling styles map opposite to see how you tend to start – and then modify – your approach in such a situation.

For example, if your first choice was Resolving and your second choice was Forcing, the shift is towards being less co-operative. Still assertive, but less co-operative. Maybe that worked. Maybe it didn't. The map will help you to see what's happening and how you tend to move through the available choices.

Conflict-handling styles map

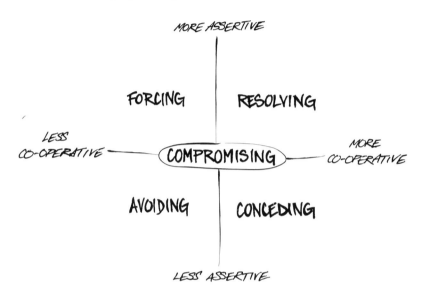

However you use it, we hope this questionnaire will help you to make sense of how you tend to behave in difficult conversations, and to ask yourself clued up questions, like:

◆ What's the context here?

◆ What's going on?

◆ What do the clues suggest?

◆ What are the politics?

◆ What are my choices?

◆ What consequences can I anticipate?

◆ What 'talking action' am I going to take?

We hope it will help you to be clued up about conflict.